SANDWICH MAKER COOKBOOK

I Love Grilled Cheese Sandwich Cookbook!

(Great Recipes You Can Make Without a Sandwich Grill)

Janice Merida

Published by Alex Howard

© **Janice Merida**

All Rights Reserved

*Sandwich Maker Cookbook: I Love Grilled Cheese Sandwich Cookbook!
(Great Recipes You Can Make Without a Sandwich Grill)*

ISBN 978-1-990169-50-2

All rights reserved. No part of this guide may be reproduced in any form without permission in writing from the publisher except in the case of brief quotations embodied in critical articles or reviews.

Legal & Disclaimer

The information contained in this book is not designed to replace or take the place of any form of medicine or professional medical advice. The information in this book has been provided for educational and entertainment purposes only.

The information contained in this book has been compiled from sources deemed reliable, and it is accurate to the best of the Author's knowledge; however, the Author cannot guarantee its accuracy and validity and cannot be held liable for any errors or omissions. Changes are periodically made to this book. You must consult your doctor or get professional medical advice before using any of the suggested remedies, techniques, or information in this book.

Table of contents

PART 1 1

INTRODUCTION 2

BEST GRILLED CHEESE 3
ASIAN SLOPPY JOES 5
CHICKEN PARM GRILLED CHEESE 7
GENERAL TSO CHICKEN SANDWICHES 9
CHICKEN SALAD SANDWICH 12
MEXICAN SHRIMP SANDWICHES 14
HOMEMADE PHILLY CHEESESTEAK 16
PIZZA GRILLED CHEESE 18
BUFFALO CHICKEN MEATBALL SUB 20
FAJITA CHICKEN SANDWICHES 22
LASAGNA GRILLED CHEESE BITES 24
SHEET PAN ITALIAN SUBS 26
BBQ PULLED CHICKEN SANDWICHES 28
HAWAIIAN GRILLED CHEESE 30
SHRIMP PO' BOY SLIDERS 32
MEXICAN HUEVOS RANCHEROS SANDWICH 34
MAPLE BOURBON CHICKEN AND WAFFLE SANDWICH 36
FRENCH DIP SLIDERS 39
GRILLED CHEESE DOGS 41
CAESAR CHICKEN SANDWICHES 43
HONEY HAM CORNBREAD SANDWICH 45
EGG IN A HOLE BLT 47
MONTE CRISTO CASSEROLE 49
FRENCH TOAST HAM AND CHEESE SANDWICHES 51
GRILLED CAPRESE CHICKEN AND CHEESE SANDWICH 53

SANDWICHES RECIPES 55

OPEN-FACED CHICKEN SANDWICHES WITH GREEN PEA SPREAD AND PARMESAN 56
B.L.A.S.T. SANDWICH 59
LOW-FAT LOBSTER ROLLS 61
GRILLED EGGPLANT PITA SANDWICHES WITH YOGURT-GARLIC SPREAD 63

Mediterranean Flatbread Sandwiches 65
Avocado Chicken Salad Sandwiches... 67
Grown-Up Grilled Cheese Sandwiches 69
Grilled BBQ Chicken Sandwiches With Spicy Avocado Spread 71
Grilled Chicken And Pineapple Sandwiches 73
Turkey Cobb Sandwiches 75
Tuscan Tuna Sandwich 77
Tarragon Chicken Salad Sandwiches With Apple 79
Pesto Chicken Salad Sandwiches... 81
Dried Cherry-Toasted Almond Turkey Salad Sandwiches...................................... 83
Chicken And Waffle Sandwiches... 85
Grilled Zucchini Caprese Sandwiches 87
Prosciutto, Pear, And Blue Cheese Sandwiches... 89
Smoked Salmon Sandwiches With Ginger Relish 91
Grilled Tomato And Brie Sandwiches.. 93
Overstuffed Grilled Vegetable-Feta Sandwiches 95
Curried Chicken Salad Sandwiches 97
Lemon-Cranberry Tuna Salad Sandwiches.. 99

CONCLUSION.. 101

PART 2.. 102

1. Mouth-Watering Tangy Turkey & Swiss Sandwiches 103
2. One Of A Kind Day After Turkey Sandwich 105
3. Delectable Bacon Turkey Bravo Sandwich 106
4. Fragrant Turkey Bacon Avocado Sandwich 107
5. Luscious Turkey Club Panini (Sandwich) 108
6. Incredible Pop's Roast Turkey Sandwich 109
7. Devil May Care Sweet & Spicy Turkey Sandwich... 110
8. Awesome Hot Roasted Turkey Mountain (Hot Turkey Sandwich) 111
9. Dynamic Garden Turkey Sandwich With Lemon Mayo................................ 112
10. Snappy Grilled Turkey Reuben Sandwiches 113
11. Stimulating Light Toasty Turkey Club Sandwich 114
12. Tasty Bennigans Monte Cristo Sandwich... 115
13. Tempting Grilled Turkey Cuban Sandwiches 117
14. Wholesome Turkey Reuben Grilled Sandwiches... 119
15. Relishing Turkey Veg Out Sandwiches 120

16. Rich Grilled Maple Turkey Sandwich 121
17. Ambrosial Toasted Salami & Turkey Sandwiches 122
18. Exquisite The Realtor's Day After Thanksgiving Turkey Sandwich 123
19. Savory Turkey BBQ Sandwiches 124
20. Eye-Opener Best Grilled Cheese & Turkey Sandwich 125
21. Scrumptious Turkey & Lingonberry Open Faced Sandwiches 126
22. Appealing Grilled Turkey & Swiss Sandwich 127
23. Delectable Summer's Smoked Turkey Sandwich 128
24. Delicious Grilled Tomato, Smoked Turkey, & Muenster Sandwich 129
25. Delish California Club Turkey Sandwich 130
26. Divine French-Toasted Ham, Turkey & Cheese Sandwich 131
27. Heavenly Tailgate Club Sandwich 133
28. Inviting Turkey & Feta Grilled Sandwich 135
29. Tantalizing Smoked Turkey Sandwich With Cranberry Butter 137
30. Yummy Smoked Turkey & Stilton Sandwich 139
31. Choice Grilled Hot Turkey Sandwiches 141
32. Tasteful Toasted Turkey & Bacon Sandwiches 143
33. Ambrosia Turkey Sandwiches With Cranberry Sauce 145
34. Tempting Turkey Tea Sandwiches 147
35. Unimaginable Mom's Sit Sandwich 149
36. A Shocker Pink Turkey Sandwich 151
37. Gotta Have It Jamaican Turkey Sandwich 152
1) The Best Ham And Cheese Sandwich 154
2) Hearty Breakfast Sandwich 156
3) Mini Pizza's With Scrambled Egg 158
4) Cheesy Buttered Breakfast Sandwich 160
5) Cheesy Baguette With Basil And Egg 162
6) Bacon, Omelette And Tomato English Muffin 164
7) Avocado And Egg Breakfast Sandwich 166
8) Energizing Egg Breakfast Sandwich 168
9) Sautéed Spinach, Mushroom And Egg Breakfast Sandwich 170
10) Sauerkraut And Egg Gluten-Free Breakfast Sandwich 172
11) Cheesy Onion And Italian Sausage Breakfast Sandwich 174
12) Cream Cheese Salmon With Spinach And Egg Breakfast Sandwich 176
13) Avocado, Arugula And Egg Sandwich 178
14) Avocado, Bacon, Tomato And Egg Breakfast Sandwich 180

15) Hash Brown Patty With Spinach And Cheese Sandwich 182
16) Hearty Meatless Breakfast Sandwich 184
17) Sausage, Bacon, And Avocado Breakfast Sandwich 185
18) Baked Egg And Spinach With Avocado Bagel Sandwich 186
19) Toasted Baguette With Mixed Greens, Avocado And Egg Sandwich 187
20) Toasted Croissants With Buttered Egg And Bean Sprouts 188
21) Asparagus With Fried Egg Breakfast Sandwich 189
22) Tangy Feta Cheese Over English Muffin 190
23) Low Calorie Breakfast Sandwich 191
24) Simple Veggie Packed Breakfast Sandwich ...... **Error! Bookmark not defined.**
25) Egg With Avocado And Aioli Spread Bagel Sandwich. **Error! Bookmark not defined.**
26) Peanut Butter, Maple Syrup And Fruits On Sandwich **Error! Bookmark not defined.**
27) Fried Egg With Reuben Sandwich .... **Error! Bookmark not defined.**
28) Israeli Style Fried Eggplant Sandwich .... **Error! Bookmark not defined.**
29) Spicy Cheesy Kale Breakfast Sandwich .... **Error! Bookmark not defined.**
30) Roasted Turkey With Cranberry Chutney Breakfast Sandwich .... **Error! Bookmark not defined.**
31) Fig With Goat Cheese In Cinnamon-Raisin Breakfast Sandwich .... **Error! Bookmark not defined.**

Part 1

Introduction

What exactly is a sandwich? A sandwich is nothing more than two slices of bread with a filling in between. The wonderful thing about sandwiches is that you can literally make them with practically every type of filling imaginable, whether you are a meat lover or a vegetarian. Not only are sandwiches easy to prepare, but they make for the perfect quick lunch or dinner snack. No matter what type of sandwich you make, a great sandwich always starts with the basics: bread, cheese and toppings.
You will learn how to make the most delicious sandwiches by the end of this cookbook. By the end of this cookbook, not only do I hope you have learned all of the basics of sandwich making, but have discovered over 25 delicious sandwich recipes that you can make any day of the week. By the end of this cookbook, I guarantee you will become a sandwich pro.
So, let's stop wasting time and get to cooking!

Best Grilled Cheese

This is one grilled cheese recipe that everyone will love once they get a taste of it. It is simple to make and can be made in just a matter of minutes.

Makes: **2 servings**
Total Prep Time: 15 minutes
Ingredients:

- 5 Tbsp. of butter, soft and divided
- 4 slices of sourdough bread
- 2 cups of cheddar cheese, shredded

Directions:
1. Spread 1 tablespoon of butter on one side of each slice of bread.
2. Flip the bread slices and spread ½ cup of cheese. Sandwich two slices of bread together.
3. In a skillet set over medium heat, add the sandwiches with the butter side facing down. Cook for

2 minutes. Flip and continue to cook for an additional 2 minutes.
4. Serve immediately.

Asian Sloppy Joes

This is a delicious twist to everybody's favorite weeknight dinner. It is so delicious, I guarantee your family will be begging for seconds.

Makes: **4 servings**
Total Prep Time: 25 minutes
Ingredients:

- 2 tsp. of sesame oil
- ½ of an onion, chopped
- 3 cloves of garlic, minced
- 1 pound of ground pork
- ½ cup of ketchup
- ½ cup of hoisin sauce
- 2 Tbsp. of low sodium soy sauce
- 2 Tbsp. of light brown sugar
- 1 Tbsp. of apple cider vinegar
- Dash of salt and black pepper
- 1 cup of cabbage, shredded
- 2 Tbsp. of mayonnaise

- ½ of a lime, juice only
- 2 Tbsp. of sesame seeds
- 2 green onions, thinly sliced
- 4 sesame buns

Directions:
1. In a skillet set over medium heat, add in the sesame oil. Add in the onions. Cook for 5 minutes or until soft. Add in the minced garlic. Cook for 30 seconds or until fragrant.
2. Add in the ground pork. Continue to cook for 8 minutes or until browned.
3. Add in the ketchup, hoisin, soy sauce, light brown sugar and vinegar. Stir well to mix. Season with a dash of salt and black pepper. Allow to come to a simmer. Cook for 5 minutes or until thick in consistency.
4. In a bowl, add in the shredded cabbage, mayonnaise and lime juice. Season with a dash of salt and black pepper. Stir well to mix.
5. Prepare the sandwiches. On the bottom half of the buns, add the sloppy joe mix. Sprinkle the sliced green onions and sesame seeds over the top. Top off with the remaining buns halves.
6. Serve immediately.

Chicken Parm Grilled Cheese

This is the ultimate grilled cheese dish for you to make whenever you are craving something incredibly cheesy. One bite and I know you will become hooked.

Makes: 1 serving
Total Prep Time: 20 minutes
Ingredients:
- 1 Tbsp. of butter
- 2 slices of sourdough bread
- 1 Tbsp. + 2 tsp. of marinara sauce
- 1 cup of mozzarella cheese, shredded and evenly divided
- ¼ cup of grated Parmesan cheese, extra for garnish
- 3 ounces of breaded chicken, cut into cubes
- Torn basil leaves
- Dash of black pepper

Directions:

1. Preheat the oven to broil.
2. Assemble the sandwich. Spread the butter onto one side of the slices of sourdough bread. On the unbuttered side of the bread, spread 1 tablespoon of the marinara sauce. Top off ¾ cup of shredded mozzarella cheese, grated Parmesan cheese, breaded chicken cubes and torn basil leaves. Top off with the remaining bread slice, with the butter side facing up.
3. In a skillet set over medium heat, add the sandwich. Cook for 5 minutes on each side or until crispy.
4. Spread the remaining 2 teaspoons of marinara sauce. Top off with the remaining ¼ cup of shredded mozzarella.
5. Transfer into the oven to broil for 2 minutes or until golden.
6. Sprinkle the remaining grated Parmesan cheese and dash of black pepper over the top.
7. Serve.

General Tso Chicken Sandwiches

One bite of this sandwich and you will never want to order from your favorite takeout spot ever again. You don't even need rice to enjoy it!

Makes: **4 servings**
Total Prep Time: 30 minutes
Ingredients for the chicken:

- 1 pound of chicken, chopped into small pieces
- ½ cup of cornstarch
- ½ cup of all-purpose flour
- Dash of salt and black pepper
- Vegetable oil, as needed

Ingredients for the sauce:

- 1 Tbsp. of sesame oil
- 2 cloves of garlic, minced
- 1 tsp. of ginger, minced
- 1 Tbsp. of cornstarch
- ¼ cup of soy sauce
- ½ cup of low sodium chicken broth

- 2 Tbsp. of apple cider vinegar
- 1 Tbsp. of hoisin sauce
- 1 Tbsp. of honey
- 2 green onions, thinly sliced
- 1 Tbsp. of sesame seeds
- 1/3 cup of mayonnaise
- Sriracha sauce, for serving
- 4 hamburger buns
- Lettuce, for serving

Directions:
1. In a bowl, add in the chicken pieces, cornstarch and all-purpose flour. Season with a dash of salt and black pepper. Toss well until the chicken is coated.
2. In a skillet set over medium heat, add in enough vegetable oil to coat the bottom. Add in the chicken. Cook for 8 to 10 minutes or until cooked through. Remove and transfer onto a plate. Season with a dash of salt and black pepper.
3. In the skillet, add in the sesame oil. Add in the minced garlic and minced ginger. Cook for 1 minute or until fragrant. Add in the cornstarch and stir well until coated.
4. Add in the chicken broth, soy sauce, vinegar, hoisin sauce and honey. Stir well to mix. Allow to come to a boil. Lower the heat to low. Cook for 2 minutes or until thick in consistency.
5. Add in the chicken. Stir well to coat in the sauce. Add in the sliced green onions and sesame seeds. Stir well to incorporate.

6. In a bowl, add in the mayonnaise and a dash of Sriracha sauce. Stir well to mix. Spread onto the bottom half of each hamburger bun.

7. Top the mayo off with the lettuce and cooked chicken. Cover with the top halves of the burger buns.

8. Serve.

Chicken Salad Sandwich

This is a delicious sandwich you can make whenever you need something simple to prepare. It is so delicious, it will make you relive some of your favorite childhood memories.

Makes: **4 servings**
Total Prep Time: 25 minutes
Ingredients:
- 3 chicken breasts, boneless and skinless
- 6 slices of lemon
- 6 sprigs of dill
- 1 green apple, chopped
- ½ of a red onion, chopped
- 2 stalks of celery, chopped
- 2/3 cup of mayonnaise
- ¼ cup of Dijon mustard
- 2 Tbsp. of red wine vinegar
- Dash of salt and black pepper
- 1 Tbsp. of dill, chopped and for garnish

- Baguette, for serving
- Butter lettuce, for serving

Directions:
1. Prepare the chicken. In a pot set over medium heat, add in the chicken breasts in a single layer. Top off with the lemon slices and sprigs of dill. Pour the water over the chicken to cover. Allow to come to a boil. Lower the heat to low. Cook for 10 minutes or until the chicken reaches an internal temperature of 165 degrees.
2. Remove the chicken and transfer onto a cutting board. Chop into small pieces. Transfer into a bowl.
3. In the bowl, add in the chopped apple, chopped onion and chopped celery. Stir well to mix.
4. In a separate bowl, add in the mayonnaise, Dijon mustard and red wine vinegar. Season with a dash of salt and black pepper. Stir well to mix. Pour over the chicken and stir well to mix.
5. Spread the chicken mix onto the baguette. Top off with the butter lettuce and dill.
6. Serve.

Mexican Shrimp Sandwiches

This is a delicious sandwich dish you can make whenever you are craving homemade shrimp. It is packed full of an authentic Mexican flavor I know you will love.

Makes: **4 servings**
Total Prep Time: 20 minutes
Ingredients:

- 1 ½ pound of shrimp, peeled and tails removed
- 2 Tbsp. of extra virgin olive oil
- 1 lime, juice only and evenly divided
- 1 tsp. of powdered garlic
- 1 tsp. of powdered chili
- ½ tsp. of powdered cumin
- Dash of salt
- ½ cup of mayonnaise
- 1 Tbsp. of hot sauce
- 4, 8 inch rolls
- 1 avocado, thinly sliced

- 2 tomatoes, thinly sliced
- 1 cup of cabbage, shredded

Directions:
1. Preheat the oven to 400 degrees. Place a sheet of parchment paper onto a baking sheet.
2. In a bowl, add in the shrimp, extra virgin olive oil, lime juice, powdered garlic, powdered chili and powdered cumin. Season with a dash of salt. Stir well to mix. Spread onto the baking sheet.
3. Place into the oven to bake for 8 to 10 minutes or until cooked through.
4. In a separate bowl, add in the remaining lime juice, mayonnaise and hot sauce. Stir well to mix. Spread onto the cut sides of the rolls.
5. Add the shrimp onto the rolls. Top off with the avocado slices, sliced tomato and shredded cabbage.
6. Serve.

Homemade Philly Cheesesteak

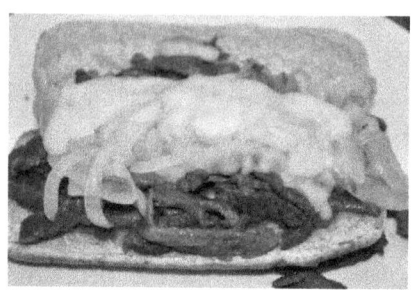

With the help of this delicious sandwich recipe, you will never have to take a trip to Philly ever again. Top with roasted peppers and smothered in plenty of cheese, this sandwich won't disappoint.

Makes: **4 servings**
Total Prep Time: 25 minutes
Ingredients:

- 2 Tbsp. of extra virgin olive oil, evenly divided
- 2 green bell peppers, thinly sliced
- 2 red bell peppers, thinly sliced
- 1 yellow onion, thinly sliced
- Dash of salt and black pepper
- 1 ½ pound of sirloin steak, thinly sliced
- 10 slices of provolone
- 4 hoagie rolls

Directions:

1. In a skillet set over medium heat, add in 1 tablespoon of olive oil. Add in the sliced red and green bell peppers. Add in the sliced yellow onion. Season with a dash of salt. Cook for 10 to 15 minutes or until caramelized.
2. Transfer the onion mix onto a plate and set aside.
3. In the skillet, add in the remaining tablespoon of olive oil. Add in the sliced steak. Cook for 5 minutes or until the steak reaches your desired doneness.
4. Add the onion mix back into the skillet. Toss to mix.
5. Cover the mix with the slices of provolone cheese. Continue to cook for 3 minutes or until the cheese is melted.
6. Divide the mix among the hoagie rolls.
7. Serve immediately.

Pizza Grilled Cheese

If you love the taste of pizza, then this is one sandwich dish I know you are going to want to make as often as possible.

Makes: 1 serving
Total Prep Time: 20 minutes
Ingredients:
- 2 Tbsp. of butter
- 2 slices of sourdough bread
- 1 Tbsp. + 2 tsp. of pizza sauce
- 1 cup of mozzarella cheese, shredded and evenly divided
- 8 slices of pepperoni, evenly divided
- 1 Tbsp. of grated Parmesan cheese, extra for garnish
- 1 basil leaf
- Crushed red pepper flakes, for garnish

Directions:
1. Preheat the oven to broil.
2. Spread butter onto one side of the slices of bread. On the inside of one bread slice, add 1 tablespoon of the pizza sauce. Top off with ¾ cup of mozzarella cheese, 5 slices of the pepperoni, grated parmesan cheese and basil. Top with the remaining bread slice with the butter side facing up.
3. In a skillet set over medium heat, add in the sandwich. Cook for 5 minutes or until crispy.
4. Spread the remaining 2 teaspoons of pizza sauce over the sandwich. Add the remaining ¼ cup of mozzarella cheese over the top followed by 3 of the pepperoni slices.
5. Transfer into the oven to broil for 2 minutes or until golden.
6. Remove and garnish with crushed red pepper flakes before serving.

Buffalo Chicken Meatball Sub

This is a classic and delicious meatball sub you can prepare in just a matter of minutes. Top off with your favorite toppings for the tastiest results.

Makes: **12 servings**

Total Prep Time: 40 minutes

Ingredients:

- ½ cup of hot sauce + 2 Tbsp. of melted butter
- 1 pound of ground chicken
- ½ cup of panko breadcrumbs
- 1 egg
- 1 stalk of celery, sliced thinly
- 1 Tbsp. of parsley, chopped
- 1 tsp. of powdered garlic
- Dash of salt and black pepper
- Hoagie rolls, for serving
- ¼ pound of pepper jack cheese slices

Directions:

1. Prepare the meatballs. Preheat the oven to 400 degrees.
2. In a bowl, add in the hot sauce, ground chicken, panko breadcrumbs, egg, sliced celery, chopped parsley and powdered garlic. Season with a dash of salt and black pepper. Stir well to mix.
3. Shape into 12 meatballs that are gold ball sized. Transfer onto a baking sheet lined with a sheet of parchment paper.
4. Place into the oven to bake for 15 to 20 minutes or until cooked through.
5. Prepare the sub. Toast the hoagie and place two slices of cheese on the bottom half of the rolls. Add 3 meatballs over the top. Add two more slices of over the meatballs. Top off with the hot sauce mix.
6. Remove and serve immediately.

Fajita Chicken Sandwiches

If you love fresh fajitas, then this is one dish I know you will love. Once you get a taste of it, you will swear that fajitas are even better on bread.

Makes: **4 servings**

Total Prep Time: 55 minutes

Ingredients:

- 3 Tbsp. of extra virgin olive oil, evenly divided
- 1 lime, juice only
- 2 tsp. of powdered cumin
- 2 tsp. of powdered chili
- Dash of cayenne pepper
- 1 pound of chicken breasts, boneless, skinless and thinly sliced
- Dash of salt and black pepper
- 1 onion, thinly sliced
- 4 red bell peppers, seeds removed and thinly sliced
- 4 slices of Monterey jack cheese
- Baguettes, toasted and for serving
- Cilantro, chopped and for garnish

- Lime wedges, for serving

Directions:
1. In a bowl, add in 2 tablespoons of olive oil, lime juice, powdered cumin, powdered chili and cayenne pepper. Stir well to mix. Add in the chicken. Season with a dash of salt and black pepper. Toss well to mix.
2. In a skillet set over medium heat, add in the remaining olive oil. Add in the sliced onion and sliced red bell peppers. Cook for 8 to 10 minutes or until soft.
3. Add in the chicken and toss well to mix. Cook for 10 minutes or until golden.
4. Add in the slices of Monterey jack cheese. Cover and cook for 2 minutes or until melted.
5. Transfer the mix onto the baguettes. Serve with a garnish of chopped cilantro a fresh lime juice.

Lasagna Grilled Cheese Bites

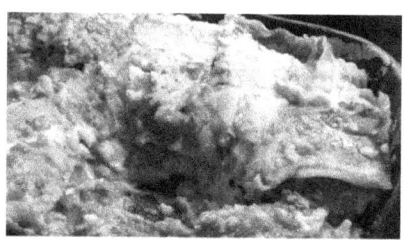

This is the perfect sandwich recipe to make that is the ultimate combination of two family favorites. Feel free to use Sourdough bread or Italian bread for this recipe.

Makes: **24 servings**
Total Prep Time: 30 minutes
Ingredients:

- ¼ cup of mayonnaise, for grilling
- 8 slices of sourdough bread
- ½, 26 ounce jar of marinara sauce
- 1, 14 ounce container of ricotta cheese
- 2 cups of mozzarella cheese, shredded

Directions:
1. Spread the mayonnaise onto one side of the bread slices. Place onto a plate with the butter side facing down.
2. Spread the marinara sauce over each slice of bread. Spread the ricotta cheese over the bread slices.

3. Sprinkle the shredded mozzarella cheese over each slice of bread. Bring two bread slices together to form a sandwich.
4. In a skillet set over medium heat, add in the sandwiches. Cook for 1 to 2 minutes or until the sandwiches are cooked through.
5. Remove and allow to rest for 10 minutes.
6. Cut into small pieces.
7. Serve with extra marinara sauce for dipping.

Sheet Pan Italian Subs

This is the perfect sandwich dish you can make whenever you want to impress your friends and family with your cooking skill.

Makes: **14 servings**
Total Prep Time: 55 minutes
Ingredients:

- 4 Tbsp. of butter, melted and evenly divided
- 2 loaves of sourdough bread
- 1 pound of deli sliced ham
- ½ pound of salami, thinly sliced
- ½ pound of mozzarella cheese, thinly sliced
- ½ pound of provolone cheese, thinly sliced
- 2 cups of baby spinach
- 1, 8 ounce jar of pepperoncini, drained and sliced

Directions:
1. Preheat the oven to 400 degrees.

2. Brush half of the butter onto a sheet pan. Add the bread in a single layer. Press down slightly to flatten.

3. Top off with the mozzarella cheese, a layer of ham slices, baby spinach, salami slices, pepperoncini and provolone slices. Add another layer of bread and brush with 2 tablespoons of butter. Place a second sheet pan on top to weigh down.

4. Transfer into the oven and bake for 10 minutes or until golden. Remove the sheet pan and continue to bake for 20 minutes or until golden.

5. Slice into squares.

6. Serve with a garnish of chopped parsley.

Bbq Pulled Chicken Sandwiches

This is the perfect sandwich recipe for you to make right in time for the summer holiday season. Make these sandwiches to spoil your friends and family.

Makes: 4 servings

Total Prep Time: 15 minutes

Ingredients:

- 2 Tbsp. of apple cider vinegar
- 1 Tbsp. of Worcestershire sauce
- ½ cup of ketchup
- 2 cloves of garlic, grated
- 1 ½ red onion, 1 onion thinly sliced and ½ an onion chopped
- Dash of salt and black pepper
- 2 Tbsp. of light brown sugar
- 1 tsp. of Dijon mustard
- 1 rotisserie chicken, shredded
- 4 sandwich buns
- 2 Tbsp. of butter, soft

- Butter pickles, for serving

Directions:
1. Preheat the oven to 350 degrees.
2. In a pot set over medium heat, add in the apple cider vinegar, Worcestershire sauce, ketchup, grated garlic and chopped onion. Stir well to mix. Cook for 5 minutes or until the onion is soft. Season with a dash of salt and black pepper.
3. Add in the light brown sugar and Dijon mustard. Allow to come to a boil. Cook for 2 minutes.
4. Add in the shredded chicken. Stir well to incorporate.
5. Toast the sandwich buns. Spoon the chicken mix onto the sandwich buns.
6. Top off with the sliced onion and butter pickles.
7. Serve immediately.

Hawaiian Grilled Cheese

One bite of the grilled cheese and you will swear you are in paradise. This grilled cheese is packed with a sweet flavor I know you will love.

Makes: **4 servings**
Total Prep Time: 10 minutes
Ingredients:

- 4 Tbsp. of butter
- 8 slices of white Hawaiian bread
- 8 slices of sharp cheddar cheese
- 4 slices of provolone cheese
- 8 pineapple rings
- 1 cup of teriyaki sauce

Directions:
1. Spread the butter onto each slice of bread.
2. In a skillet set over medium heat, add the bread slices with the butter side facing down. Top off the bread slices with 2 slices of cheddar cheese, 1 slice of provolone cheese, 2 pineapple rings and ¼ cup of

teriyaki sauce. Top off with the second slice of bread with the butter side facing up.
3. Cook for 4 minutes on each side or until golden.
4. Remove and serve immediately.

Shrimp Po' Boy Sliders

Po' Boys are a classic in the south and now with the help of this recipe, you can bring this popular dish to your home.

Makes: **12 servings**
Total Prep Time: 30 minutes
Ingredients:

- ½ cup of whole milk
- 2 eggs
- ½ cup of all-purpose flour
- ½ cup of powdered cornmeal
- 1 Tbsp. of Cajun seasoning
- 1 tsp. of dried thyme
- Dash of salt and black pepper
- Vegetable oil, for frying
- 1 pound of shrimp, peeled and tails removed
- 12 slider buns
- Iceberg lettuce, shredded and for serving
- Cherry tomatoes, sliced and for serving

Ingredients for the remoulade:
- 1 cup of mayonnaise
- 1 Tbsp. of whole grain mustard
- 1 Tbsp. of lemon juice
- 1 Tbsp. of hot sauce
- 1 Tbsp. of parsley, chopped
- 2 green onions, thinly sliced

Directions:
1. In a bowl, add in the whole milk and eggs. Whisk until mixed. In a separate bowl, add in the all-purpose flour, cornmeal, Cajun seasoning and dried thyme. Stir to mix. Season with a dash of salt and black pepper.
2. Dredge the shrimp in the milk mix. Add into the flour mix and toss well until coated.
3. In a skillet set over medium heat, add in 2 inches of vegetable oil. Add in the shrimp. Fry for 2 to 3 minutes or until golden. Remove and transfer onto a plate lined with paper towels to drain.
4. Prepare the remoulade. In a bowl, add in the mayonnaise, mustard, lemon juice, hot sauce, chopped parsley and sliced green onions. Stir well to mix.
5. Spread the remoulade onto the bottom sides of the slider buns. Top off with the fried shrimp, shredded lettuce and sliced cherry tomatoes. Top
with the top portion of the slider buns.
6. Serve immediately.

Mexican Huevos Rancheros Sandwich

This is a delicious sandwich you can make for breakfast, lunch or dinner. It is the great dish to make whenever you need to kick off your day in a delicious way.
Makes: **1 serving**
Total Prep Time: 20 minutes
Ingredients for the syrup:
- ¾ cup of light brown sugar
- ½ cup of water
- ½ cup of whole cloves
- 1 orange, peeled
- 4 sticks of cinnamon
- 1 almond, chopped

Ingredients for the sandwich:
- ¼ cup of refried beans
- ½ tsp. of powdered chili
- 2 tsp. of extra virgin olive oil
- 1 soft sandwich roll, toasted
- 1 egg, fried
- ¼ of an avocado, thinly sliced

- 2 slices of bacon, crispy
- Hot sauce, for garnish
- Cilantro, chopped and for garnish

Directions:
1. Prepare the syrup. In a pot set over medium to high heat, add in all of the ingredients for the syrup. Whisk well to mix. Allow to come to a boil. Cook for 6 minutes or until reduced. Remove from heat.
2. Strain the mix into a jar. Set aside to cool.
3. Prepare the sandwich. In a bowl, add in the refried beans, powdered chili and olive oil. Stir well to mix. Spread onto both sides of the toasted roll.
4. On the bottom side of the roll, add in the fried egg, avocado and bacon. Drizzle hot sauce over the top. Top off with the chopped cilantro.
5. Serve immediately.

Maple Bourbon Chicken And Waffle Sandwich

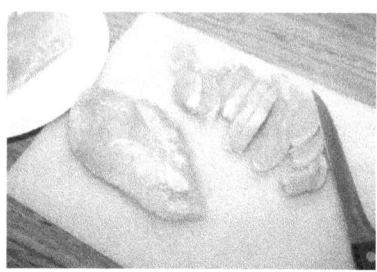

This is a no-fuss sandwich you can make that is perfect to enjoy nearly every morning. Topped off with chicken, bacon and maple syrup, this is a delicious sandwich that will kick off your morning the right way.

Makes: **4 servings**
Total Prep Time: 30 minutes
Ingredients for the waffles:

- 3 eggs, separated
- 2 boxes of cornbread mix
- ½ cup of all-purpose flour
- ½ cup of baker's style baking soda
- 1 cup of whole milk
- 2 Tbsp. of honey
- 4 Tbsp. of butter, melted

Ingredients for the chicken:

- 1 pound of chicken cutlets, sliced in half
- 1 cup of buttermilk
- 1 Tbsp. of hot sauce
- 1 ½ cups of all-purpose flour

- 2 tsp. of powdered garlic
- 1 tsp. of smoked paprika
- Dash of salt and black pepper
- Vegetable oil, for frying

Ingredients for the maple syrup:
- 2 ounces of bourbon whiskey
- 8 ounces of maple syrup
- 3 Tbsp. of butter

Directions:
1. Prepare the waffles. Preheat the waffle iron.
2. In a bowl, add in the egg whites. Beat with an electric mixer until peaks begin to form. Set aside.
3. In a separate bowl, add in the cornbread mix, egg yolks, all-purpose flour, whole milk, honey, melted butter and baking soda. Stir well to mix. Add into the egg whites and stir well until just mixed.
4. Pour ½ cup of the batter into the waffle iron. Close the lid. Cook for 5 minutes or until golden. Remove and repeat.
5. Prepare the chicken. In a bowl, add in the butter and hot sauce. Whisk to mix. Ad in the chicken and stir to mix. Set aside.
6. In a separate bowl, add in the all-purpose flour, powdered garlic and smoked paprika. Season with a dash of salt and black pepper. Stir well to mix.
7. Dredge the chicken in the flour mix.
8. In a skillet set over medium to high heat, add in 1 inch of vegetable oil. Once hot, add in the chicken

cutlets. Cook for 5 minutes or until golden. Transfer onto a plate and set aside to drain.

9. Prepare the syrup. In a saucepan set over medium to high heat, add in the bourbon and maple syrup. Cook for 5 minutes or until reduced. Remove and add in the butter. Whisk to mix. Remove and set aside to cool.

10. Assemble the sandwiches. Add a piece of fried chicken in between two of the waffles. Drizzle the bourbon sauce over the top.

11. Serve immediately.

French Dip Sliders

Don't be fooled by the size of these sliders. While they may be small, they pack a major flavor punch that will leave you craving for more.

Makes: 1 serving
Total Prep Time: 45 minutes
Ingredients:

- 12 slider buns, cut into halves
- 2 onions, thinly sliced
- ¼ tsp. of powdered garlic
- 2 sprigs of thyme
- Dash of salt and black pepper
- 1 pound of deli style roast beef
- 12 slices of provolone cheese
- 2 Tbsp. of butter, melted
- Dash of sea salt
- 1 Tbsp. of parsley, chopped

Ingredients for the au jus:

- 1 Tbsp. of butter

- 1 clove of garlic, minced
- 1 ½ cup of beef stock
- 1 Tbsp. of Worcestershire sauce
- ¼ tsp. of thyme leaves

Directions:
1. Preheat the oven to 350 degrees. Place the bottom half of the slider buns onto a baking sheet.
2. In a skillet set over medium to high heat, add in the butter. Add in the onion and thyme sprigs. Cook for 5 minutes or until the onions are golden. Season with a dash of salt and black pepper.
3. Reduce the heat to medium. Continue to cook for 10 to 15 minutes or until the onions are caramelized. Remove from heat.
4. Prepare the sliders. On the bottom half of the slider buns, add the caramelized onion, roast beef and provolone cheese. Place the remaining slider tops over the top. Brush with the melted butter. Sprinkle the powdered garlic, sea salt and chopped parsley over the top.
5. Place into the oven to bake for 10 to 15 minutes. Remove and set aside.
6. Prepare the au jus. In a skillet set over medium heat, add the butter. Add in the minced garlic. Cook for 1 minute or until fragrant. Add in the beef stock, Worcestershire sauce and the thyme leaves. Season with a dash of salt and black pepper. Continue to cook for 10 minutes or until slightly reduced.
7. Serve the sliders with the au jus sauce for dipping.

Grilled Cheese Dogs

If you love the taste of hot dogs and grilled cheese, then this is one dish I know you are going to love. This is a sandwich dish that combines them both to make the ultimate lunch or dinner.

Makes: **4 servings**
Total Prep Time: 25 minutes
Ingredients:
- 4 hot dog buns
- 2 Tbsp. of butter, soft
- ¼ tsp. of powdered garlic
- ¼ tsp. of powdered onion
- 4 hot dogs, sliced
- 3 cups of cheddar cheese, shredded
- Green onions, thinly sliced and for garnish

Directions:
1. Flatten the hot dogs with rolling pin.

2. In a bowl, add in the butter, powdered garlic and powdered onion. Stir well to mix. Spread on the bottom of the buns.

3. In a skillet set over medium heat, add in the hot dogs. Cook for 2 minutes on both sides or until charred. Remove and set aside.

4. Place the buns into the skillet with the buttered side. Top off with ½ cup of shredded cheddar cheese. Top off with the charred hot dog. Sprinkle the shredded cheddar cheese and sliced green onions.

5. Cover the skillet. Cook for 1 to 2 minutes or until the cheese melts. Remove and set aside.

6. Serve immediately.

Caesar Chicken Sandwiches

This is a delicious sandwich dish that you don't have to feel guilty about enjoying. Once you get a taste of it, I know you will want to make it for lunch as often as possible.

Makes: **6 servings**
Total Prep Time: **4 hours and 10 minutes**
Ingredients:
- 2 cups of creamy Caesar dressing, extra for serving
- 1 cup of chicken broth
- 1 pound of chicken breasts, boneless and skinless
- 1 Tbsp. of lemon juice
- 2 cloves of garlic, minced
- 1 cup of grated Parmesan cheese
- 1 head of romaine lettuce, chopped
- 4 ciabatta rolls
- 1 Tbsp. of butter

- Shaved parmesan cheese, for serving

Directions:
1. In a slow cooker, add in the Caesar dressing, chicken broth, chicken breasts, lemon juice and minced garlic. Toss gently to mix.
2. Season with a dash of salt and black pepper.
3. Cover and cook on the highest setting for 3 to 4 hours.
4. Drain out most of the liquid. Shred the chicken and toss again to mix. Add in extra Caesar dressing if you wish.
5. Top the bottom halves of the ciabatta rolls with the romaine lettuce, chicken mix and shaved parmesan cheese. Top off with the top portions of the ciabatta rolls.
6. Serve immediately.

Honey Ham Cornbread Sandwich

This toasted sandwich is the perfect combination of salty and sweet flavors that you will love. Make this whenever you are craving something different.

Makes: **4 servings**
Total Prep Time: 35 minutes
Ingredients:

- 1 box of corn muffin mix
- 2 eggs
- ¼ cup of canola oil
- ¼ cup of honey
- 1 tsp. of powdered mustard
- ½ pound of country ham, thinly sliced
- ¼ pound of Swiss cheese slices
- Spicy pickles, for serving

Directions:
1. Preheat the oven to 350 degrees.

2. In a bowl, add in the corn muffin mix, eggs, canola oil, honey and powdered mustard. Stir well to mix.

3. Grease a sheet pan with cooking spray. Line with a sheet of parchment paper. Pour the cornbread mix onto the pan.

4. Place into the oven to bake for 15 minutes or until golden. Remove and set aside to cool completely. Slice into 8 pieces.

5. Place a few slices of ham and cheese slices onto 4 slices of cornbread. Top off with the remaining cornbread slices.

6. Place back into the oven to bake for 1 to 2 minutes or until the cheese melts.

7. Serve immediately with the spicy pickles.

Egg In A Hole Blt

This is a delicious breakfast dish you can make whenever you are craving something light and filling for lunch.

Makes: **1 serving**
Total Prep Time: 20 minutes
Ingredients:

- 3 slices of bacon
- 2 slices of sourdough bread
- 1 egg
- 1 Tbsp. of butter
- Dash of salt and black pepper
- 2 Tbsp. of mayonnaise
- 2 slices of lettuce
- ½ of tomato, thinly sliced

Directions:

1. In a skillet set over medium heat, add in the bacon. Cook for 5 minutes or until crispy. Transfer onto a plate lined with paper towels to drain.
2. Wipe the skillet clean.
3. Use a glass and cut out a circle from one slice of bread.
4. Place the skillet back over medium heat, add in the butter. Once melted, add in the bread. Cook for 2 minutes or until toast. Flip and toast for an additional minute. Crack the egg into the hole. Season with a dash of salt and black pepper. Cook for 5 minutes or until the whites of the eggs are cooked through.
5. Spread the remaining bread slice with mayonnaise. Top off with the lettuce, cooked bacon and sliced tomato. Season with a dash of salt and black pepper.
6. Top off with the egg in a hole bread.
7. Serve immediately.

Monte Cristo Casserole

If you need to make a dish to feed a large group of people, then look no further. Once your guests try this sandwich dish, I guarantee it will disappear in a matter of a few minutes.

Makes: **1 serving**
Total Prep Time: 45 minutes
Ingredients:
- Butter, for greasing
- 16 slices of white sandwich bread
- 1 pound of deli ham
- 2 cups of Gruyere cheese, shredded
- 6 eggs
- 2/3 cup of whole milk
- 1 tsp. of salt
- ½ tsp. of black pepper
- ¼ tsp. of powdered nutmeg
- Powdered sugar, for sprinkling

- Raspberry preserves, for serving

Directions:
1. Heat the oven to 375 degrees. Grease a baking dish with cooking spray or the butter.
2. Place the slices of white bread into the bottom of the baking dish.
3. Fold the ham slices in half and place on top of the bread slices. Sprinkle 2/3 of the cheese over the ham. Top off with the remaining bread slices.
4. In a bowl, add in the eggs, whole milk, powdered nutmeg, dash of salt and black pepper. Whisk to mix and pour over the sandwiches in the baking dish.
5. Top off with the remaining cheese.
6. Place into the oven to bake for 35 minutes or until golden on the top.
7. Remove from the oven. Sprinkle the powdered sugar and raspberry preserves over the top of the casserole.
8. Serve.

French Toast Ham And Cheese Sandwiches

This is a decadent sandwich dish I know you will love. It is made with simple bread but packed full of a delicious flavor you won't be able to resist.

Makes: **4 servings**
Total Prep Time: 25 minutes
Ingredients for the French toast:

- 3 eggs
- ½ cup of whole milk
- 1 Tbsp. of white sugar
- Dash of salt
- Dash of powdered nutmeg
- Butter, for greasing
- 4 slices of brioche bread

Ingredients for the sandwiches:

- Dijon mustard, for spreading
- 12 slices ham
- 1 cup of grated Gruyere cheese

Directions:

1. Prepare the French toast. In a bowl, add in the eggs, whole milk, white sugar, dash of salt and powdered nutmeg. Whisk well to mix.

2. In a skillet set over medium heat, add in the butter to coat the bottom of the skillet. Dip a slice of the brioche bread into the egg mix. Transfer into the skillet. Cook for 2 minutes on each side or until golden. Transfer onto a wire rack.

3. Prepare the sandwiches. Preheat the oven to broil.

4. Spread the French bread slices with Dijon mustard. Top off with three slices of ham and the grated gruyere cheese. Transfer onto a baking sheet.

5. Place into the oven to broil for 2 minutes or until toasted.

6. Remove and serve immediately.

Grilled Caprese Chicken And Cheese Sandwich

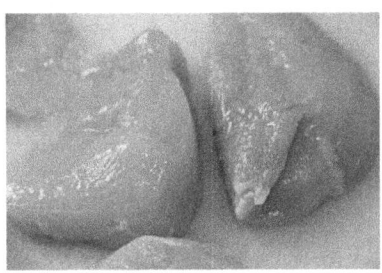

This is a delicious sandwich you can make whenever you are craving authentic Italian cuisine. One bite and you will never want to make boring regular grilled cheese ever again.

Makes: **2 servings**
Total Prep Time: 30 minutes
Ingredients:

- 2 Tbsp. of extra virgin olive oil
- 1 chicken breast, boneless and skinless
- 1 tsp. of powdered garlic
- 1 Tbsp. of Italian seasoning
- Dash of salt and black pepper
- 2 Tbsp. of butter, evenly divided
- 4 slices of sourdough bread
- 2 cups of mozzarella cheese, shredded
- 1 plum tomato, thinly sliced
- 6 basil leaves, torn
- Balsamic glaze, for serving

Directions:
1. In a skillet set over medium heat, add in the olive oil. Add in the chicken breasts. Season with the powdered garlic, Italian seasoning, dash of salt and black pepper. Cook for 8 minutes on each side or until cooked through. Remove and set aside to rest for 5 minutes. Thinly slice and set aside.
2. Spread the butter onto both sides of the bread slices.
3. Top off the bread slices with the cooked chicken, mozzarella cheese, torn basil, tomato slices and the remaining slices of bread. Repeat.
4. In a skillet set over medium heat, add in 1 tablespoon of butter. Once frothy, add in the sandwiches. Cook for 3 minutes on both sides or until the bread is golden.
5. Remove and serve immediately with the balsamic glaze.

Sandwiches Recipes

Open-Faced Chicken Sandwiches With Green Pea Spread And Parmesan

Nutritional Information
Yield: Serves 4 (serving size: 1 sandwich)
Amount per serving
Calories: 334
Fat: 15.5g
Saturated fat: 3.3g
Monounsaturated fat: 9.1g
Polyunsaturated fat: 1.8g
Protein: 24.1g
Carbohydrate: 24.4g
Fiber: 3.2g
Cholesterol: 52mg
Iron: 2.4mg
Sodium: 688mg
Calcium: 121mg
Ingredients
Cooking spray

1 (10-ounce) skinless, boneless chicken breast, halved lengthwise
1/2 teaspoon salt, divided
1/2 teaspoon black pepper, divided
1 1/2 cups frozen green peas
2 tablespoons chopped parsley
3 tablespoons plus 1/2 teaspoon extra-virgin olive oil, divided
2 tablespoons water
2 garlic cloves
1/4 teaspoon grated lemon rind
3 1/2 teaspoons fresh lemon juice, divided
1/8 teaspoon ground red pepper
4 (1-ounce) slices sourdough bread
1 cup arugula
1 ounce Parmesan cheese, shaved (about 1/4 cup)

Preparation

1. Preheat broiler to high.
2. Heat a grill pan over medium-high heat; coat with cooking spray. Sprinkle chicken evenly with 1/4 teaspoon salt and 1/4 teaspoon black pepper; cook 5 minutes on each side or until done. Remove from pan; thinly slice.
3. Combine peas, parsley, 3 tablespoons oil, 2 tablespoons water, and garlic in a small saucepan. Bring to a simmer; cook 2 minutes. Place pea mixture, rind, 1 tablespoon juice, remaining 1/4 teaspoon salt, and red pepper in a mini food processor; process until smooth.

4. Broil bread slices 1 minute on each side or until toasted. Combine arugula, remaining 1/2 teaspoon oil, and remaining 1/2 teaspoon juice. Spread pea mixture evenly over bread slices; top with arugula mixture and chicken. Sprinkle with Parmesan cheese and remaining 1/4 teaspoon black pepper.

B.L.A.S.T. Sandwich

Nutritional Information
Yield: Serves 1 (serving size: 1 sandwich)
Amount per serving
Calories: 296
Fat: 11.1g
Saturated fat: 2.5g
Monounsaturated fat: 4.8g
Polyunsaturated fat: 2.7g
Protein: 18.9g
Carbohydrate: 32.1g
Fiber: 6.3g
Cholesterol: 32mg
Iron: 2.2mg
Sodium: 870mg
Calcium: 71mg
Ingredients
3 (1-ounce) slices Canadian bacon
2 (1-ounce) slices whole-wheat bread, toasted

2 teaspoons reduced-fat mayonnaise
1 large romaine lettuce leaf
2 (1/4-inch-thick) slices beef-steak tomato
5 peeled avocado slices (about 1/4 medium avocado)

Preparation

1. Cook bacon in a small nonstick skillet over medium heat 2 minutes on each side, or until golden. Remove from pan.

2. Spread 1 side of each toast slice with 1 teaspoon mayonnaise. Layer lettuce, bacon, tomato, and avocado over mayonnaise on 1 toast slice. Cover with remaining toast slice, mayonnaise side down.

Low-Fat Lobster Rolls

Nutritional Information
Yield: Makes 4 servings
Amount per serving
Calories: 210
Calories from fat: 0.0%
Fat: 6g
Saturated fat: 1g
Monounsaturated fat: 0.0g
Polyunsaturated fat: 0.0g
Protein: 16g
Carbohydrate: 25g
Fiber: 4g
Cholesterol: 43mg
Iron: 0.0mg
Sodium: 559mg
Calcium: 0.0mg
Ingredients
8 ounces chopped cooked lobster meat
2 tablespoons reduced-fat mayonnaise

2 tablespoons minced celery
2 teaspoons minced fresh chives
1/2 teaspoon lemon zest
2 teaspoons fresh lemon juice
1/8 teaspoon salt
Pinch of freshly ground black pepper
4 whole wheat hot dog buns
Butter-flavored cooking spray
8 Bibb lettuce leaves
2 Roma tomatoes, thinly sliced

Preparation

1. Combine first 8 ingredients in a medium bowl. Cover and chill until ready to serve.
2. Heat a large nonstick skillet over medium heat. Lightly spray insides of buns with butter-flavored cooking spray, and place, sprayed sides down, in skillet. Cook 1 to 2 minutes or until golden brown.
3. Layer buns evenly with lettuce leaves, tomato slices, and lobster mixture.

Grilled Eggplant Pita Sandwiches With Yogurt-Garlic Spread

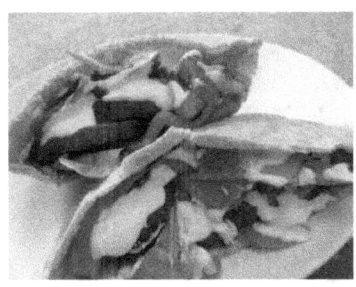

Nutritional Information
Yield: 4 servings (serving size: 2 pita halves)
Amount per serving
Calories: 311
Fat: 8.2g
Saturated fat: 1.6g
Monounsaturated fat: 5g
Polyunsaturated fat: 1.2g
Protein: 12.7g
Carbohydrate: 50.6g
Fiber: 9.2g
Cholesterol: 1.7mg
Iron: 3.5mg
Sodium: 697mg
Calcium: 117mg

Ingredients

2 (1-pound) eggplant, cut crosswise into 1/2-inch-thick slices
3 1/2 teaspoons kosher salt, divided
1/2 cup plain reduced-fat Greek-style yogurt
2 tablespoons fresh lemon juice
2 teaspoons chopped fresh oregano leaves
1/8 teaspoon black pepper
2 small garlic cloves, minced
1 small red onion, cut into 1/2-inch-thick slices
2 tablespoons extra-virgin olive oil
Cooking spray
4 (6-inch) pitas, cut in half
2 cups arugula

Preparation

1. Place eggplant slices in a colander; sprinkle with 1 tablespoon salt. Toss well. Drain 30 minutes. Rinse thoroughly; pat dry with paper towels.
2. Combine remaining 1/2 teaspoon salt, yogurt, and next 4 ingredients (through garlic) in a small bowl.
3. Preheat grill to medium-high heat.
4. Brush eggplant and onion slices with oil. Place eggplant and onion slices on grill rack coated with cooking spray; grill 5 minutes on each side or until vegetables are tender and lightly browned.
5. Fill each pita half with 1 1/2 tablespoons yogurt mixture, one quarter of eggplant slices, one quarter of onion slices, and 1/4 cup arugula.

Mediterranean Flatbread Sandwiches

Nutritional Information
Yield: 6 servings (serving size: 1/2 sandwich)
Amount per serving
Calories: 310
Calories from fat: 0.0%
Fat: 12.2g
Saturated fat: 3.4g
Monounsaturated fat: 6.6g
Polyunsaturated fat: 1.8g
Protein: 11.1g
Carbohydrate: 39.2g
Fiber: 6g
Cholesterol: 11mg
Iron: 1mg
Sodium: 549mg
Calcium: 80mg
Ingredients

1 (8.5-ounce) package 7-grain pilaf (such as Seeds of Change)
1 cup diced English cucumber
1 cup chopped seeded tomato (1 medium)
1/2 cup (2 ounces) crumbled feta cheese
2 tablespoons fresh lemon juice
1 tablespoon olive oil
1/4 teaspoon salt
1/4 teaspoon freshly ground black pepper
1 (7-ounce) container hummus (such as Athenos Original)
3 (2.8-ounce) Mediterranean-style white flatbreads (such as Toufayan)

Preparation

1. Combine first 8 ingredients in a bowl.
2. Spread hummus evenly over each flatbread.
3. Spoon pilaf mixture evenly over half of each flatbread; fold flatbread over filling.
4. Cut each sandwich in half, and serve immediately.

Avocado Chicken Salad Sandwiches

Nutritional Information
Yield: 4 servings (serving size: 1 sandwich)
Amount per serving
Calories: 364
Calories from fat: 0.0%
Fat: 16.4g
Saturated fat: 2.7g
Monounsaturated fat: 7.9g
Polyunsaturated fat: 3g
Protein: 41.4g
Carbohydrate: 24.1g
Fiber: 11.9g
Cholesterol: 95mg
Iron: 4.4mg
Sodium: 647mg
Calcium: 322mg
Ingredients
3 cups (1/2-inch) cubed cooked chicken breast
1/4 cup light mayonnaise

2 tablespoons chopped fresh cilantro
1/4 teaspoon salt
1/8 teaspoon black pepper
1 cup (1/2-inch) cubed avocado (about 1)
4 green leaf lettuce leaves
8 whole wheat bread slices, toasted

Preparation

1. Combine first 5 ingredients in a large bowl. Gently stir avocado into chicken mixture until combined.

2. Place 1 lettuce leaf onto each of 4 bread slices. Spoon chicken mixture evenly onto each lettuce leaf. Top with remaining bread slices.

Grown-Up Grilled Cheese Sandwiches

Nutritional Information
Yield: 4 servings (serving size: 1 sandwich)
Amount per serving
Calories: 376
Fat: 11g
Saturated fat: 5.3g
Monounsaturated fat: 4.8g
Polyunsaturated fat: 0.6g
Protein: 20.2g
Carbohydrate: 50.3g
Fiber: 3.3g
Cholesterol: 24mg
Iron: 2.9mg
Sodium: 876mg
Calcium: 308mg
Ingredients
Cooking spray
1 cup vertically sliced red onion
1 large garlic clove, minced

1 cup (4 ounces) shredded reduced-fat sharp white cheddar cheese (such as Cracker Barrel)
8 (1 1/2-ounce) slices hearty white bread (such as Pepperidge Farm)
2 cups fresh spinach leaves
8 (1/4-inch-thick) slices tomato
6 slices center-cut bacon, cooked

Preparation

1. Heat a large nonstick skillet over medium-low heat. Coat pan with cooking spray. Add 1 cup onion and garlic; cook for 10 minutes or until tender and golden brown, stirring occasionally.
2. Sprinkle 2 tablespoons cheese over each of 4 bread slices. Top each slice with 1/2 cup spinach, 2 tomato slices, 2 tablespoons onion mixture, and 1 1/2 bacon slices. Sprinkle each with 2 tablespoons cheese; top with the remaining 4 bread slices.
3. Heat skillet over medium heat. Coat pan with cooking spray. Place sandwiches in pan, and cook for 3 minutes on each side or until golden brown and cheese melts.

Grilled Bbq Chicken Sandwiches With Spicy Avocado Spread

Nutritional Information
Yield: 4 servings (serving size: 1 sandwich & about 2 1/2 tablespoons spicy avocado spread)
Amount per serving:
Calories: 368
Calories from fat: 39%
Fat: 16g
Saturated fat: 5g
Monounsaturated fat: 5.1g
Polyunsaturated fat: 2.3g
Protein: 31.9g
Carbohydrate: 31.8g
Fiber: 7.8g
Cholesterol: 64mg
Iron: 3.9mg
Sodium: 678mg
Calcium: 423mg
Ingredients

4 (3-ounce) skinless, boneless chicken breast cutlets
1/4 cup barbecue sauce (such as Sticky Fingers Memphis Original)
Cooking spray
4 (0.7-ounce) slices 2% reduced-fat sharp cheddar cheese
Green leaf lettuce leaves (optional)
Tomato slices (optional)
4 (1.8-ounce) white wheat hamburger buns

* **Spicy Avocado Spread** *

Ingredients :
1 ripe peeled avocado, coarsely mashed
1 tablespoon minced jalapeño pepper
1 tablespoon minced red onion
1 1/2 tablespoons fresh lime juice
1 garlic clove, pressed
2 teaspoons minced fresh cilantro
1/8 teaspoon salt
Preparation :
1. Combine all ingredients in a small bowl, stirring well.

Preparation

1. Preheat grill.
2. Brush both sides of chicken with barbecue sauce. Place chicken on grill rack coated with cooking spray. Grill 3 to 4 minutes on each side or until chicken is done, placing 1 cheese slice on each chicken breast during last minute of cooking.
3. Place lettuce and tomato on bottom half of each bun, if desired; add 1 chicken breast. Top each with

about 2 1/2 tablespoons Spicy Avocado Spread. Place remaining bun halves on top.

Grilled Chicken And Pineapple Sandwiches

Nutritional Information
Yield: 4 servings (serving size: 1 sandwich)
Amount per serving
Calories: 333
Calories from fat: 11%
Fat: 4g
Saturated fat: 0.9g
Monounsaturated fat: 1g
Polyunsaturated fat: 1.4g
Protein: 43.4g
Carbohydrate: 30.5g
Fiber: 4.1g
Cholesterol: 99mg
Iron: 2.5mg
Sodium: 608mg
Calcium: 75mg
Ingredients

4 (6-ounce) skinless, boneless chicken breast halves
1/2 teaspoon salt
1/4 teaspoon freshly ground black pepper
Cooking spray
1/4 cup fresh lime juice (about 2 limes)
4 (1/2-inch-thick) slices fresh pineapple
4 (1.5-ounce) whole wheat hamburger buns, toasted
Light mayonnaise (optional)
4 large basil leaves

Preparation

1. Prepare grill.
2. Sprinkle chicken evenly with salt and pepper. Place chicken on grill rack coated with cooking spray; grill 5 to 6 minutes on each side or until done, brushing occasionally with lime juice. Grill pineapple 2 to 3 minutes on each side or until browned.
3. Spread mayonnaise on bottom halves of buns, if desired. Top each with 1 chicken breast half, 1 pineapple slice, 1 basil leaf, and 1 bun top. Serve immediately.

Turkey Cobb Sandwiches

Nutritional Information
Yield: 4 servings (serving size: 1 sandwich)
Amount per serving
Calories: 319
Calories from fat: 42%
Fat: 14.9g
Saturated fat: 2.7g
Monounsaturated fat: 5.9g
Polyunsaturated fat: 1.9g
Protein: 22.1g
Carbohydrate: 32.1g
Fiber: 12.9g
Cholesterol: 126mg
Iron: 3.5mg
Sodium: 712mg
Calcium: 25mg
Ingredients
2 tablespoons reduced-fat mayonnaise

8 (1-ounce) slices double-fiber wheat bread (such as Nature's Own), toasted
4 small green leaf lettuce leaves
4 tomato slices
6 ounces shaved deli turkey
1 peeled avocado, sliced
4 precooked bacon slices
2 hard-cooked large eggs, sliced

Preparation

1. Spread 1/2 tablespoon mayonnaise evenly over each of 4 bread slices. Layer each evenly with lettuce and remaining ingredients. Top with remaining 4 bread slices. Cut each sandwich in half diagonally.

Tuscan Tuna Sandwich

Nutritional Information
Yield: 4 servings (serving size: 1 sandwich)
Amount per serving
Calories: 292
Calories from fat: 31%
Fat: 10g
Saturated fat: 1.6g
Monounsaturated fat: 5.6g
Polyunsaturated fat: 1.7g
Protein: 25.2g
Carbohydrate: 24.3g
Fiber: 3.3g
Cholesterol: 36mg
Iron: 2.4mg
Sodium: 878mg
Calcium: 85mg
Ingredients
1/4 cup finely chopped fennel bulb

1/4 cup pre-chopped red onion
1/4 cup chopped fresh basil
2 tablespoons drained capers
2 tablespoons fresh lemon juice
2 tablespoons extra-virgin olive oil
1/4 teaspoon black pepper
2 (6-ounce) cans solid white tuna in water, drained
1 (4-ounce) jar chopped roasted red bell peppers, drained
8 (1-ounce) slices sourdough bread, toasted

Preparation

1. Combine chopped fennel, red onion, 1/4 cup basil, capers, lemon juice, olive oil, 1/4 teaspoon black pepper, tuna, and bell peppers in a bowl, stirring well.
2. Spoon 1/2 cup tuna mixture on each of 4 bread slices. Top each serving with 1 bread slice. Cut each sandwich in half diagonally.

Tarragon Chicken Salad Sandwiches With Apple

Nutritional Information
Yield: 4 servings (serving size: 1 sandwich)
Amount per serving
Calories: 356
Calories from fat: 18%
Fat: 7.3g
Saturated fat: 2.2g
Protein: 28.5g
Carbohydrate: 45.3g
Fiber: 1.9g
Cholesterol: 61mg
Iron: 3mg
Sodium: 762mg
Calcium: 55mg
Ingredients
1 tablespoon chopped shallots
1 tablespoon plus 1 teaspoon tarragon vinegar
1/2 cup reduced-fat mayonnaise
1/2 teaspoon Dijon mustard
1 tablespoon chopped fresh tarragon

2 cups chopped cooked chicken breast
1 (8.5-ounce) loaf French bread baguette, cut diagonally into 4 equal pieces
4 red leaf lettuce leaves
1 medium Granny Smith apple, cored and thinly sliced
12 shaved pieces Parmigiano-Reggiano cheese (about 0.4 ounces)

Preparation

1. Combine shallots and tarragon vinegar in a small bowl; let stand 10 minutes. Add mayonnaise, mustard, and tarragon; stir well to combine. Reserve 3 tablespoons mayonnaise mixture. Add chicken to remaining mayonnaise mixture; stir well.

2. Spread about 2 teaspoons reserved mayonnaise mixture on bottom half of each baguette portion. Top each with 1 lettuce leaf. Divide apple slices and shaved cheese evenly among sandwiches. Top each sandwich evenly with 1/2 cup chicken salad and remaining bread half. Chill until ready to serve.

Pesto Chicken Salad Sandwiches

Nutritional Information
Yield: 10 servings (serving size: 1 sandwich)
Amount per serving
Calories: 324
Calories from fat: 28%
Fat: 10g
Saturated fat: 1.2g
Monounsaturated fat: 0.6g
Polyunsaturated fat: 2.2g
Protein: 26.4g
Carbohydrate: 31.6g
Fiber: 1.6g
Cholesterol: 55mg
Iron: 2.3mg
Sodium: 725mg
Calcium: 39mg
Ingredients
1/2 cup low-fat mayonnaise
1/3 cup plain fat-free yogurt
1/3 cup commercial pesto (such as Buitoni)
1 1/2 tablespoons fresh lemon juice

1/2 teaspoon salt
1/2 teaspoon black pepper
4 cups cubed skinless, boneless rotisserie chicken breast
1 cup diced celery
1/3 cup chopped walnuts, toasted
1 (1-pound) focaccia bread, cut in half horizontally, toasted, and cut into 20 slices
1 (12-ounce) bottle roasted red bell peppers, drained and chopped
10 romaine lettuce leaves

Preparation

1. Combine first 6 ingredients in a large bowl, stirring with a whisk. Stir in chicken, celery, and walnuts.
2. Spread 1/2 cup of salad onto each of 10 bread slices. Top each serving with about 2 tablespoons bell pepper, 1 lettuce leaf, and one bread slice.

Dried Cherry-Toasted Almond Turkey Salad Sandwiches

Nutritional Information
Yield: 4 servings (serving size: 2 stuffed pita halves)
Amount per serving
Calories: 398
Calories from fat: 20%
Fat: 8.7g
Saturated fat: 1.4g
Monounsaturated fat: 4.1g
Polyunsaturated fat: 2.4g
Protein: 25.9g
Carbohydrate: 56.1g
Fiber: 6.9g
Cholesterol: 51mg
Iron: 3.5mg
Sodium: 501mg
Calcium: 93mg
Ingredients
1/4 cup slivered almonds (about 1 ounce)

1/4 cup plain fat-free yogurt
3 tablespoons low-fat mayonnaise
1 teaspoon bottled ground fresh ginger (such as Spice World)
1/8 teaspoon crushed red pepper
3/4 cup thinly sliced celery
1/4 cup chopped red onion
1/4 cup dried cherries
1/4 cup golden raisins
8 ounces roasted turkey breast, chopped
4 (6-inch) whole wheat pitas, cut in half

Preparation

1. Heat a small nonstick skillet over medium-high heat. Add almonds; cook 2 minutes or until toasted, stirring constantly. Remove from heat; set aside.

2. Combine yogurt, mayonnaise, ginger, and pepper in a medium bowl. Add almonds, celery, and next 4 ingredients (through turkey), stirring well to combine. Spoon 1/3 cup turkey mixture into each pita half.

Chicken And Waffle Sandwiches

Nutritional Information
Yield: Serves 4
Amount per serving
Calories: 355
Fat: 19.5g
Saturated fat: 2g
Monounsaturated fat: 7.6g
Polyunsaturated fat: 7.4g
Protein: 16.3g
Carbohydrate: 33.5g
Fiber: 6.6g
Cholesterol: 39mg
Iron: 2mg
Sodium: 739mg
Calcium: 32mg
Ingredients
4 slices lower-sodium bacon, halved crosswise
3 tablespoons canola mayonnaise
1 tablespoon low-fat buttermilk
1 teaspoon cider vinegar

1/4 teaspoon sugar
1/4 teaspoon garlic powder
1/8 teaspoon freshly ground black pepper
8 frozen whole-grain waffles, toasted
6 ounces thinly sliced, lower-sodium deli chicken breast
8 (1/4-inch-thick) slices ripe tomato
4 Boston lettuce leaves

Preparation

1. Cook bacon in a large nonstick skillet over medium heat until crisp. Drain on paper towels.

2. Combine mayonnaise and the next 5 ingredients (through black pepper) in a small bowl.

3. Spread mayonnaise mixture evenly over 4 waffles. Divide chicken, bacon, tomato, and lettuce evenly among servings. Top with remaining waffles.

Grilled Zucchini Caprese Sandwiches

Nutritional Information
Yield: 4 servings (serving size: 1 sandwich)
Amount per serving
Calories: 343
Fat: 16.8g
Saturated fat: 6.6g
Monounsaturated fat: 8g
Polyunsaturated fat: 1.3g
Protein: 15.4g
Carbohydrate: 35.3g
Fiber: 2g
Cholesterol: 33.6mg
Iron: 2.3mg
Sodium: 722mg
Calcium: 229mg

Ingredients
1 medium zucchini, trimmed and cut lengthwise into 6 slices
4 teaspoons extra-virgin olive oil, divided

1 garlic clove, minced
1 1/2 teaspoons balsamic vinegar
1/8 teaspoon kosher salt
1/8 teaspoon black pepper
4 (2-ounce) ciabatta rolls, split and toasted
8 large fresh basil leaves
1 medium tomato, thinly sliced
6 ounces fresh mozzarella cheese, thinly sliced

Preparation

1. Heat a large grill pan over medium-high heat. Place zucchini in a shallow dish. Add 2 teaspoons oil and garlic; toss to coat. Arrange zucchini in grill pan; cook 2 minutes on each side or until grill marks appear. Cut each zucchini piece in half crosswise. Return zucchini to shallow dish. Drizzle with vinegar. Sprinkle with salt and black pepper.

2. Brush bottom halves of rolls with the remaining 2 teaspoons oil. Top evenly with zucchini, basil, tomatoes, and mozzarella.

3. Brush cut side of roll tops with remaining liquid from shallow dish, and place on sandwiches. Heat the sandwiches in pan until warm.

Prosciutto, Pear, And Blue Cheese Sandwiches

Nutritional Information
Yield: 4 servings (serving size: 1 sandwich)
Amount per serving
Calories: 324
Fat: 13.8g
Saturated fat: 5.4g
Monounsaturated fat: 5g
Polyunsaturated fat: 0.8g
Protein: 15g
Carbohydrate: 36.4g
Fiber: 9.7g
Cholesterol: 26mg
Iron: 2.1mg
Sodium: 706mg
Calcium: 408mg

Ingredients
8 slices 100% multigrain bread
1 tablespoon butter, softened
3 cups arugula

1 medium shallot, thinly sliced
1 tablespoon extra-virgin olive oil
2 teaspoons red wine vinegar
1/8 teaspoon freshly ground black pepper
2 ounces thinly sliced prosciutto
1 ripe pear, cored and thinly sliced
2 ounces blue cheese, sliced

Preparation

1. Preheat broiler.
2. Arrange bread in a single layer on a baking sheet; broil 3 minutes or until toasted. Turn bread slices over; spread butter evenly over bread slices. Broil an additional 2 minutes or until toasted.
3. Combine arugula and shallot in a medium bowl. Drizzle arugula mixture with oil and vinegar; sprinkle with pepper. Toss well to coat. Divide arugula mixture evenly among 4 bread slices, buttered side up; top evenly with prosciutto. Divide pear slices and cheese evenly among sandwiches; top each sandwich with 1 bread slice, buttered side down.

Smoked Salmon Sandwiches With Ginger Relish

Nutritional Information
Yield: 4 servings (serving size: 1 sandwich)
Amount per serving
Calories: 267
Fat: 2.2g
Saturated fat: 0.3g
Monounsaturated fat: 1.1g
Polyunsaturated fat: 0.4g
Protein: 14g
Carbohydrate: 45.6g
Fiber: 4g
Cholesterol: 7mg
Iron: 3.5mg
Sodium: 702mg
Calcium: 62mg

Ingredients
2 (7-ounce) cucumbers, peeled, seeded, and cut into chunks
1 (8-ounce) daikon radish, peeled and cut into chunks

4 green onions, cut into 2-inch pieces
1 (1-inch) piece fresh ginger, peeled and coarsely chopped
1/4 cup rice vinegar
1 teaspoon sugar
1 teaspoon lower-sodium soy sauce
1 (16-ounce) whole-wheat baguette, cut in half lengthwise
12 large fresh spinach leaves
1/4 pound thinly sliced cold-smoked salmon

Preparation

1. Place cucumbers in a food processor; pulse 15 times or until finely chopped. Place in a large bowl. Add radish to food processor; pulse 15 times or until finely chopped. Add radish to bowl. Add green onions and ginger to food processor; process until minced. Add to bowl.

2. Combine vinegar, sugar, and soy sauce; stir until sugar dissolves. Pour over cucumber mixture; let stand at least 15 minutes. Drain in a fine mesh sieve, pressing to squeeze out excess moisture.

3. Preheat broiler.

4. Hollow out top and bottom halves of bread, leaving a 1/2-inch-thick shell; reserve torn bread for another use. Place bread on a baking sheet, cut sides up; broil 3 minutes or until toasted. Layer spinach, salmon, and relish on bottom half of bread; cover with top half of bread. Cut into 4 equal pieces.

Grilled Tomato And Brie Sandwiches

Nutritional Information
Yield: 4 servings (serving size: 1 sandwich)
Amount per serving
Calories: 234
Fat: 10.1g
Saturated fat: 5.1g
Monounsaturated fat: 3.1g
Polyunsaturated fat: 1g
Protein: 11g
Carbohydrate: 26.9g
Fiber: 6.5g
Cholesterol: 28mg
Iron: 1.8mg
Sodium: 445mg
Calcium: 210mg
Ingredients
8 (1-ounce) slices 100% whole-grain bread (about 1/4 inch thick)
1 teaspoon olive oil

1 garlic clove, halved
2 teaspoons country-style Dijon mustard
4 ounces Brie cheese, thinly sliced
1 1/3 cups packaged baby arugula and spinach greens (such as Dole)
8 (1/4-inch-thick) slices beefsteak tomato
Cooking spray

Preparation

1. Prepare grill to high heat.
2. Brush one side of each bread slice with oil; rub cut sides of garlic over oil. Spread 1/2 teaspoon mustard on each of 4 bread slices, oil side down. Top each bread slice with 1 ounce cheese, 1/3 cup greens, and 2 tomato slices. Top each with remaining 4 bread slices, oil side up.
3. Place sandwiches on grill rack coated with cooking spray; grill 2 minutes on each side or until lightly toasted and cheese melts.

Overstuffed Grilled Vegetable-Feta Sandwiches

Nutritional Information
Yield: 4 servings (serving size: 1 piece)
Amount per serving
Calories: 283
Calories from fat: 25%
Fat: 8g
Saturated fat: 3.5g
Monounsaturated fat: 1.2g
Polyunsaturated fat: 0.7g
Protein: 11.6g
Carbohydrate: 42.5g
Fiber: 3.2g
Cholesterol: 19mg
Iron: 2.7mg
Sodium: 773mg
Calcium: 158mg

Ingredients
1 1/3 cups refrigerated pre-sliced yellow squash and zucchini mix

4 (1/4-inch-thick) slices red onion
Cooking spray
3/4 cup grape tomatoes, halved
3 tablespoons light Northern Italian salad dressing with basil and Romano (such as Ken's Steak House Lite)
1 tablespoon chopped fresh basil
1 (8-ounce) loaf French bread, halved lengthwise
3/4 cup (3 ounces) crumbled feta cheese

Preparation

1. Prepare grill.
2. Coat squash mix and onion evenly with cooking spray. Place vegetables on grill rack; grill 4 minutes on each side or until crisp-tender and beginning to brown.
3. Place tomato in a medium bowl; add dressing and basil, tossing gently to coat. Add cooked vegetables to tomato mixture; toss well.
4. Coat cut sides of bread with cooking spray. Grill bread 1 minute on each side or until lightly toasted. Spoon vegetable mixture over bottom half of bread; sprinkle evenly with cheese. Top with remaining bread half. Press down lightly; cut crosswise into 4 equal pieces.

Curried Chicken Salad Sandwiches

Nutritional Information
Yield: 8 servings (serving size: 1 sandwich)
Amount per serving
Calories: 321
Fat: 14.1g
Saturated fat: 2.1g
Protein: 32.4g
Carbohydrate: 28.4g
Cholesterol: 65mg
Iron: 4.1mg
Sodium: 626mg
Calories from fat: 40%
Fiber: 10.9g
Calcium: 339mg
Ingredients
1/2 cup light mayonnaise
1/4 cup plain low-fat yogurt
1 teaspoon curry powder
1 teaspoon lemon juice
1/2 teaspoon salt

4 cups shredded cooked chicken breast
1/2 cup seedless red grapes, halved
1/2 cup chopped walnuts, toasted
1 (8-ounce) can pineapple tidbits in juice, drained
1/3 cup diced red onion
16 slices whole wheat double-fiber bread (such as Nature's Own)
8 lettuce leaves

Preparation

1. Combine first 5 ingredients in a large bowl. Add chicken and next 4 ingredients; stir well to combine.

2. Top each of 8 bread slices with 1/2 cup chicken salad. Top each with a lettuce leaf and a bread slice.

Lemon-Cranberry Tuna Salad Sandwiches

Nutritional Information
Yield: 4 servings (serving size: 1 sandwich)
Amount per serving
Calories: 301
Fat: 6.5g
Saturated fat: 2.1g
Protein: 19.4g
Carbohydrate: 40.0g
Cholesterol: 32mg
Iron: 2.6mg
Sodium: 678mg
Calories from fat: 20%
Fiber: 2.8g
Calcium: 101mg
Ingredients
1/3 cup fat-free mayonnaise
1/4 cup low-fat sour cream
1/4 cup sweetened dried cranberries, coarsely chopped
1 tablespoon chopped fresh dill

1/2 teaspoon freshly ground black pepper
1/4 teaspoon grated lemon rind
1 teaspoon fresh lemon juice
1 (12-ounce) can solid white tuna in water, drained
8 basil leaves
4 (2-ounce) kaiser rolls, sliced in half horizontally
1 small cucumber, sliced
8 Bibb lettuce leaves

Preparation

1. Combine first 7 ingredients in a medium bowl; stir in tuna.
2. Place 2 basil leaves on bottom halves of each roll; top basil leaves evenly with tuna mixture. Top each sandwich with cucumber slices, 2 lettuce leaves, and tops of rolls.

Conclusion

Well, there you have it!

Hopefully by the end of this book you have found plenty of sandwich recipes that you can make with ease. By the end of this sandwich cookbook, not only do I hope you have gained the confidence to try new sandwich recipes you have never had before, but also have found plenty of sandwich recipes to satisfy your picky taste buds.

So, what is next for you?

The next step for you to take is to begin making all of the sandwich recipes you have discovered inside of this cookbook. Once you have done that, it will be time for you to research even more sandwich recipes to make from home.

Good luck!

Part 2

1. Mouth-Watering Tangy Turkey & Swiss Sandwiches

Yield: Makes 4 Servings
Ingredients:
3/4 cup chopped red onion
1 tablespoon dried thyme
1/2 cup mayonnaise
1/4 cup coarse-grain brown mustard
8 slices country style French Bread
6 tablespoons butter, softened
1 pound thinly sliced roast turkey
8 slices tomato
8 slices Swiss cheese

To Make:
Step 1. In a small bowl, stir together the red onion, thyme, mayonnaise and mustard.
Step 2. Spread some of this mixture onto one side of each slice of bread.
Step 3. Spread butter onto the other side of the slices of bread.
Step 4. Heat a large skillet over medium heat. Place 4 slices of the bread into the skillet with the butter side down.
Step 5. On each slice of bread, layer 1/4 of the sliced turkey, then 2 slices of tomato, and top with 2 slices of Swiss cheese.
Step 6. Place remaining slices of bread over the top with the butter side up.

Step 7. When the bottoms of the sandwiches are golden brown, flip over, and cook until golden on the other side.

2. One Of A Kind Day After Turkey Sandwich

Yield: Makes 1 Serving
Ingredients:
leftover turkey slice
left over prepared stuffing
left over cranberry sauce
mayonnaise (the real stuff)
white bread (wonder is the best)
salt & pepper
To Make:
Step 1. Put a lot of mayo on the nice, fresh, soft wonder bread.
Step 2. Add the turkey slices, stuffing and cranberry sauce.
Step 3. Some salt & pepper and Enjoy!

3. Delectable Bacon Turkey Bravo Sandwich

Yield: Makes 1 Serving
Ingredients:
Dressing:
1 cup mayonnaise
1/2 cup ketchup
2 tablespoons lemon juice, freshly squeezed
1/2 teaspoon dried mustard
1 teaspoon Worcestershire sauce
1 dash Tabasco sauce
Sandwich:
2 slices tomato basil bread (or other hearty favorite)
1 leaf romaine lettuce
3 slices tomatoes (1/4-inch thick)
4 ounces smoked turkey breast, sliced thin
1 slice smoked gouda cheese
2 slices bacon, cooked crisp
To Make:
Dressing:
Step 1. Combine all the ingredients in a small bowl and stir well.
Step 2. Refrigerate.
This makes 1 3/4 cups, and will keep a long time in the fridge.
Sandwich:
Step 1. Spread 2 tbsp. of the dressing on one of the bread slices (we put it on both sides).
Step 2. On top of one slice of bread, layer lettuce, tomato, turkey, Gouda, and bacon.

Step 3. Top with the second slice of bread and serve.

4. Fragrant Turkey Bacon Avocado Sandwich

Yield: Makes 1 Serving
Ingredients:
1 tablespoon reduced-fat mayonnaise (optional)
2 slices bread, toasted
1 slice provolone cheese
4 thin slices deli turkey breast
4 slices precooked bacon, microwaved according to package directions
1/2 avocado - peeled, pitted, and thinly sliced
1 slice ripe tomato
To Make:
Step 1. Spread mayonnaise on one side of both slices of toasted bread.
Step 2. Top a bread slice with provolone cheese, turkey, bacon, avocado, tomato, and lettuce.
Step 3. Place the remaining bread slice on top, slice in half, and serve.

5. Luscious Turkey Club Panini (Sandwich)

Yield: Makes 1 Serving
Ingredients:
2 slices Texas toast thick bread
3 ounces deli turkey, sliced thin
1 slice bacon, cooked crisp
2 slices tomatoes
mayonnaise
1 slice Swiss cheese (I use light)
drizzle olive oil or butter-flavored cooking spray

To Make:
Step 1. Assemble sandwich using all ingredients except oil.
Step 2. Brush oil on bread or spray with butter.
Step 3. Cook until sandwich is crisp on the outside and cheese has melted.

6. Incredible Pop's Roast Turkey Sandwich

Yield: Makes 1 Serving
Ingredients:
2 slices cinnamon raisin bread, toasted
1 teaspoon unsalted butter or 1 teaspoon margarine, to taste
2 -4 slices cooked turkey (thick slices)
1/2 teaspoon apricot jam, to taste
1/2 teaspoon mayonnaise, to taste
1 -2 slice Havarti cheese, thinly sliced
2 slices granny smith apples, thinly sliced
2 large lettuce leaves
To Make:
Step 1. Lightly toast the bread and spread with butter to taste.
Step 2. Roll up the turkey into logs and place on one piece of bread.
Step 3. Top with cheese, apple slices, and lettuce.
Step 4. Spread apricot jam and mayo onto the other slice of bread and place on top of the other slice.
Step 5. Poke a toothpick on each side of the sandwich to hold it together, then cut through the center, on a slight diagonal.

7. Devil May Care Sweet & Spicy Turkey Sandwich

Yield: Makes 1 Serving
Ingredients:
2 slices (1/2 inch thick) hearty country bread
4 slices roasted turkey breast
1 slice Pepper Jack cheese
2 teaspoons butter
4 teaspoons strawberry preserves
To Make:
Step 1. Heat a small skillet over medium heat.
Step 2. Butter one side of each of the bread slices with one teaspoon butter.
Step 3. Place one slice, butter side down, in the skillet.
Step 4. Top with the turkey and cheese slices.
Step 5. Place the second slice of bread on top, butter side up.
Step 6. When the first side of the sandwich is golden brown, turn and brown the other side, 3 to 5 minutes per side, or until the cheese begins to melt.
Step 7. Remove sandwich to a plate and top with strawberry preserves, or serve the preserves on the side.

8. Awesome Hot Roasted Turkey Mountain (Hot Turkey Sandwich)

Yield: Makes 6 Servings
Ingredients:
1 (6 ounce) package chicken flavor stuffing mix or 1 (6 ounce) package turkey stuffing mix
3 tablespoons butter or 3 tablespoons margarine
water
6 slices bread, toasted
1 lb. cooked turkey breast, sliced
1 1/2-2 cups turkey gravy (jarred or homemade) or 1 1/2-2 cups chicken gravy, heated (jarred or homemade)
To Make:
Step 1. Prepare stuffing mix as directed on package, using only 3 tablespoons butter or margarine.
Step 2. Set aside.
Step 3. Place 1 toast slice on each of six individual plates.
Step 4. Top evenly with turkey, stuffing and gravy.
Step 5. Microwave to reheat, if desired.
Step 6. Microwave, one serving at a time, on High 30 sec. or just until warmed.

9. Dynamic Garden Turkey Sandwich With Lemon Mayo

Yield: Makes 1 Serving
Ingredients:
1 teaspoon lemon peel, grated
1 tablespoon low-fat mayonnaise
2 slices whole grain bread
1 cup baby spinach leaves, loosely packed
2 ounces cooked turkey breast, sliced
1 small tomatoes, sliced
To Make:
Step 1. Stir lemon peel into mayonnaise.
Step 2. Spread on both slices of bread.
Step 3. Layer half of spinach leaves, turkey, tomato slices, and remaining spinach leaves on one slice of bread.
Step 4. Top with second slice of bread.

10. Snappy Grilled Turkey Reuben Sandwiches

Yield: Makes 2 Servings
Ingredients:
1 cup sauerkraut, drained
10 ounces sliced deli turkey meat
2 tablespoons butter
4 slices marble rye bread
4 slices Swiss cheese
4 tablespoons thousand island salad dressing, or to taste

To Make:
Step 1. Warm the sauerkraut and turkey, separately, in a microwave-safe bowls for 30-seconds; set aside.
Step 2. Spread butter generously on one side of each slice of rye bread, then spread the thousand island dressing on the other side.
Step 3. Divide the sauerkraut, turkey, and Swiss cheese on two slice of bread with the butter-side down.
Step 4. Stack the remaining two slices of bread with the butter-side up on top.
Step 5. Heat a large skillet over medium-low heat.
Step 6. Arrange the sandwiches on the skillet and grill until lightly browned and the cheese is melted, about 3 minutes on each side.

11. Stimulating Light Toasty Turkey Club Sandwich

Yield: Makes 1 Serving
Ingredients:
2 slices light bread (40-45 calories each with about 2g fiber per slice)
2 slices lean turkey bacon or 2 slices center-cut bacon
4 -6 slices 98% fat free oven-roasted turkey breast
2 slices tomatoes
2 leaves romaine lettuce
2 teaspoons fat-free mayonnaise
To Make:
Step 1. Toast the bread.
Step 2. Cut bacon strips in half.
Step 3. Over medium heat, cook bacon strips in a pan sprayed with nonstick spray until crispy (about 5 minutes).
Step 4. Spread mayo onto one piece of bread, and then top with the turkey slices, tomato, lettuce, and bacon.
Step 5. Finish it all off with the other piece of bread and eat!

12. Tasty Bennigans Monte Cristo Sandwich

Yield: Makes 3 Servings
Ingredients:
9 slices whole wheat bread
3 slices cooked turkey
3 slices cooked ham
3 slices American cheese
3 slices Swiss cheese
Batter:
1 egg
1 -1 1/4 cup water
1/2 teaspoon salt
1 teaspoon sugar
1 1/2 cups flour
1 tablespoon baking powder
vegetable oil (for deep frying)
To Make:
Step 1. Place turkey and Swiss cheese on one slice of bread and ham and American cheese on another slice of bread.
Step 2. Place third slice in-between and secure the triple-decker sandwich in the corners with tooth picks.
Step 3. Place egg in mixing bowl, add water and beat together.
Step 4. Add salt, sugar, flour, and baking powder.
Step 5. Beat batter until smooth.
Step 6. Dip sandwich in batter and carefully cover all the sides and surface.
Step 7. Carefully place in hot oil and fry until golden.

Step 8. When sandwich has turned a warm gold color remove from hot oil and place on paper towel.

Step 9. Let cool for a few minutes before removing the tooth picks.

Step 10. Before serving slice into fourths and sprinkle with powder sugar.

Step 11. Serve with Raspberry jam.

13. Tempting Grilled Turkey Cuban Sandwiches

Yield: Makes 6 Servings
Ingredients:
Non-stick cooking spray
1 (3 pound) Butterball® Boneless Breast of Turkey Roast, thawed
2 cloves garlic, peeled, sliced
1 tablespoon canola oil
1 tablespoon ground cumin
2 teaspoons salt
1 teaspoon coarsely ground black pepper
2 loaves Cuban, French or Italian bread (15 inches long)
1/4 cup honey mustard
1/2 pound smoked ham
1/2 pound sliced Swiss cheese
12 sandwich-style dill pickle slices
To Make:
Step 1. Spray cold grate of outdoor gas grill with cooking spray.
Step 2. Prepare grill for medium indirect heat.
Step 3. Remove turkey from package.
Step 4. Dry with paper towels.
Step 5. Discard gravy packet or refrigerate for another use (within 2 - 3 days).
Step 6. Lift string netting and shift position on roast for easier removal after cooking.
Step 7. Cut small slits, at least 1 inch apart, over entire surface of turkey.
Step 8. Insert 1 garlic slice into each slit.

Step 9. Brush turkey with oil.
Step 10. Combine cumin, salt and pepper.
Step 11. Sprinkle over turkey.
Step 12. Place turkey on grill grate over drip pan.
Step 13. Cover grill with lid.
Step 14. Grill 1 1/4 to 1-3/4 hours, or until meat thermometer reaches 170 degrees F when inserted into center of roast.
Step 15. Remove from grill.
Step 16. Let stand 10 minutes.
Step 17. Remove string netting.
Step 18. Cut half of the turkey into six 1/8-inch-thick slices.
Step 19. Set aside.
Step 20. Refrigerate unsliced turkey for another use.
Step 21. Cut each bread loaf lengthwise in half.
Step 22. Then, cut each into 3 pieces (for 6 sandwiches).
Step 23. Spread the bottom half of each section with 2 teaspoons mustard.
Step 24. Top with the sliced turkey, ham, cheese and pickles.
Step 25. Cover with tops of bread loaves.
Step 26. Press sandwiches with hands to flatten.
Step 27. Tightly wrap individually in aluminum foil.
Step 28. Place wrapped sandwiches on grill grate.
Step 29. Top each with heavy iron skillet or brick.
Step 30. Grill 3 to 5 minutes on each side, or until heated through.

Step 31. Serve sandwiches warm, wrapped in aluminum foil.

14. Wholesome Turkey Reuben Grilled Sandwiches

Yield: Makes 4 Servings
Ingredients:
4 tablespoons thousand island dressing, divided (I use nonfat Kraft)
3/4 cup sauerkraut
8 slices dark pumpernickel bread
1 teaspoon caraway seed
4 slices Swiss cheese (I use low fat)
8 ounces turkey breast
cooking spray
To Make:
Step 1. Spread dressing on one side of each slice of the bread.
Step 2. Layer sandwiches: turkey breast, sauerkraut, caraway seeds and cheese.
Step 3. Cover with a second piece of bread.
Step 4. Heat a nonstick skillet to med-high; lightly coat with cooking spray.
Step 5. Place sandwich in pan.
Step 6. Cook 1 minute.

Step 7. Spray top side of sandwich, flip and cook an additional minute until crispy and cheese is melted.

Step 8. Cool slightly and cut in half.

15. Relishing Turkey Veg Out Sandwiches

Yield: Makes 6 Servings
Ingredients:
1/2 cup yellow squash, sliced and diced
1/2 cup red pepper, sliced and diced
1/2 cup green pepper, sliced and diced
1/2 cup broccoli, sliced and diced
1/2 cup Bermuda onion, sliced and diced
1/2 cup zucchini, sliced and diced
1/2 cup fat-free chicken broth
6 onion rolls, unsliced
6 ounces lean turkey breast
1 tomatoes, sliced into 6 slices
3 ounces provolone cheese, sliced into 6 slices
To Make:
Step 1. Sauté or steam vegetables in chicken broth.
Step 2. Take a thin slice from the top of each roll and scoop out the center leaving about 1/4 inch around the sides.
Step 3. Fill rolls with the drained vegetables.
Step 4. Top each sandwich with 1 oz. of turkey, a slice of tomato and a slice of cheese.
Step 5. Spray a baking sheet with non-stick cooking spray and place sandwiches on tray.
Step 6. Cook under broiler until the cheese melts.
Step 7. Serve with soup or a fruit salad for a pretty and tasty luncheon.

My mother uses the filling in tortillas and rolls them up instead of using the onion rolls.

16. Rich Grilled Maple Turkey Sandwich

Yield: Makes 1 Serving
Ingredients:
3 strips bacon
4 ounces sliced deli-style maple turkey
2 tablespoons butter, softened
2 slices raisin black bread
4 slices Swiss cheese
2 tablespoons honey mustard
To Make:
Step 1. Place bacon into a skillet over medium heat, and cook until crisp.
Step 2. Remove, and drain on paper towels.
Step 3. Drain bacon grease from skillet.
Step 4. Add maple turkey to the skillet, and cook briefly, just long enough to heat through.
Step 5. Butter both sides of the bread. Layer one slice with two slices of the Swiss cheese, then layer with the maple turkey, and the bacon.
Step 6. Drizzle with honey mustard, and top with remaining two slices of Swiss cheese.
Step 7. Top with remaining bread slice, and cut sandwich in half.
Step 8. Return sandwich halves to the skillet, and cook over medium heat, turning once, until cheese begins to melt, 4 to 5 minutes.

17. Ambrosial Toasted Salami & Turkey Sandwiches

Yield: Makes 2 Servings
Ingredients:
2 pub-style sandwich buns
1-2 tablespoon butter or 1-2 tablespoon margarine
1 slice mozzarella cheese
1 slice cheddar cheese
4 slices salami or 4 slices pepperoni
5 slices deli turkey or 5 slices deli chicken
1 tablespoon mayonnaise (optional)
1 tablespoon mustard (optional)
To Make:
Step 1. Butter both halves of the buns.
Step 2. Broil in the oven until just turning brown.
Step 3. Remove from oven.
Step 4. Add cheese to the top half of the bun.
Step 5. Add turkey and salami to bottom half of bun.
Step 6. Return to oven and broil until cheese just melted.
Step 7. Remove from oven and add mayonnaise and mustard if desired.

18. Exquisite The Realtor's Day After Thanksgiving Turkey Sandwich

Yield: Makes 1 Serving
Ingredients:
1 fresh croissant, split
3 slices roast turkey
1/2 cup prepared stuffing
mayonnaise
2 tablespoons cranberry sauce (whole or jellied)
red leaf lettuce (or other leafy lettuce- we like Romain)
To Make:
Step 1. Spread the inside of the split croissant with mayonnaise or warmed gravy.
Step 2. Heat the turkey and stuffing in the microwave on HIGH for 30 seconds, if desired.
Step 3. Layer half of croissant with hot turkey and stuffing, cranberry sauce and lettuce, and top with the other half of croissant.
Step 4. Serve immediately.

19. Savory Turkey Bbq Sandwiches

Yield: Makes 6 Servings
Ingredients:
2 turkey legs without skin
1/2 cup firmly packed brown sugar
1/4 cup prepared yellow mustard
1 tablespoon liquid smoke flavoring
2 tablespoons ketchup
2 tablespoons apple cider vinegar
2 tablespoons hot pepper sauce
1 teaspoon salt
1 teaspoon coarse ground black pepper
1 teaspoon crushed red pepper flakes

To Make:

Step 1. Spray the inside of a slow cooker with nonstick cooking spray, and place the turkey legs into the cooker.

Step 2. In a bowl, mix together the brown sugar, yellow mustard, smoke flavoring, ketchup, cider vinegar, hot pepper sauce, salt, black pepper, and red pepper flakes until the sugar has dissolved.

Step 3. Pour the mixture over the turkey legs.

Step 4. Cover the cooker, set to Low, and cook 8 to 10 hours.

Step 5. Remove the turkey legs from the cooker, separate meat from bones and tendons, and shred the meat; return the meat to the sauce for serving.

20. Eye-Opener Best Grilled Cheese & Turkey Sandwich

Yield: Makes 1 Serving
Ingredients:
2 slices whole wheat bread
2 slices provolone cheese
2 slices turkey, buffalo style from the deli
2 teaspoons fat-free mayonnaise
To Make:
Step 1. Heat a nonstick pan over medium high heat.
Step 2. Spread one side of each slice of bread with a tsp of mayo, coating it evenly.
Step 3. Place one slice in the pan, mayo side down.
Step 4. Arrange meat and cheese on the bread with the meat between the slices of cheese.
Step 5. Place the other slice of bread on top with mayo side up.
Step 6. Cover and cook to desired toasting level.
Step 7. Flip and repeat.

21. Scrumptious Turkey & Lingonberry Open Faced Sandwiches

Yield: Makes 4 Servings

Ingredients:
4 slices bread, Lingonberry or 4 slices rye meal
4 teaspoons butter, at room temperature
2 teaspoons Dijon mustard
1 dash dill weed
4 lettuce leaves
8 ounces cooked turkey breast, sliced
1/4 cup lingonberry preserves

To Make:

Step 1. Spread bread with butter and mustard; sprinkle on a dill weed.

Step 2. Place lettuce leaf on each piece of bread, top with the sliced turkey, and garnish with a dollop of lingonberry preserves.

22. Appealing Grilled Turkey & Swiss Sandwich

Yield: Makes 1 Serving
Ingredients:
1 tablespoon mayonnaise
2 slices thick-cut rye bread
2 slices Swiss cheese
2 slices leftover turkey meat, or to taste
1/4 cup baby spinach, or to taste
To Make:
Step 1. Set oven rack about 6 inches from the heat source and preheat the oven's broiler.
Step 2. Spread mayonnaise onto 1 side of each bread slice.
Step 3. Layer Swiss cheese, turkey, and spinach onto the mayonnaise-side of 1 bread slice; top with second bread slice.
Step 4. Place sandwich on a baking sheet.
Step 5. Broil in the preheated oven until heated through and cheese is bubbling, about 5 minutes.

23. Delectable Summer's Smoked Turkey Sandwich

Yield: Makes 1 Serving
Ingredients:
2 slices country bread
1 teaspoon mayonnaise
3 1/2 ounces thinly sliced smoked turkey
1/2 ripe jersey tomatoes, sliced thin
3 large fresh basil leaves
dill pickle slices
To Make:
Step 1. Spread one slice of the bread with a teaspoon of mayonnaise.
Step 2. Layer on the turkey, tomato slices and basil.
Step 3. Top with the remaining bread slice and cut in half.
Step 4. Garnish with pickles.

24. Delicious Grilled Tomato, Smoked Turkey, & Muenster Sandwich

Yield: Makes 2 Servings
Ingredients:
1 tablespoon minced red onion
3 tablespoons nonfat sour cream
1 tablespoon Dijon mustard
1 teaspoon chopped fresh thyme or 1/4 teaspoon dried thyme
4 teaspoons butter, softened
4 slices sourdough bread
6 slices fat-free honey roasted turkey breast
4 slices tomatoes
2 slices muenster cheese
To Make:
Step 1. Combine the first 4 ingredients in a bowl.
Step 2. Spread 1 teaspoon butter on one side of each bread slice.
Step 3. Spread 2 tablespoons mustard mixture over unbuttered side of each of 2 bread slices; top each with 3 turkey slices, 2 tomato slices, 1 cheese slice, and 1 bread slice (with buttered side out).
Step 4. Heat a large nonstick skillet over medium heat until hot.
Step 5. Add the sandwiches; cover and cook for 3 minutes on each side or until golden brown.

25. Delish California Club Turkey Sandwich

Yield: Makes 1 Serving
Ingredients:
1 tablespoon cream cheese, or to taste
2 slices toasted whole wheat bread
1 tablespoon sunflower seeds
3 slices avocado
1 teaspoon mayonnaise
3 slices smoked turkey, or to taste
To Make:
Step 1. Spread cream cheese on one piece of toast.
Step 2. Sprinkle sunflower seeds over the cream cheese and place avocado slices over the seeds.
Step 3. Spread mayonnaise on the other piece of toast.
Step 4. Arrange turkey slices over the mayonnaise.
Step 5. Put turkey side of sandwich together with the avocado side of the sandwich.

26. Divine French-Toasted Ham, Turkey & Cheese Sandwich

Yield: Makes 6 Servings
Ingredients:
12 slices bread (use French or Italian white or rye bread)
prepared yellow mustard (use as much as you want)
6 slices ham, thinly sliced
6 slices chicken or 6 slices turkey, thinly sliced
6 slices Swiss cheese (use thin slices) or 6 slices cheddar cheese (use thin slices)
3 eggs, slightly beaten
1 cup milk
1/2 teaspoon salt
black pepper
softened butter (for the bread and frying)

Make To:

Step 1. Spread the inside of each slice of bread with prepared mustard.

Step 2. In a shallow dish combine the milk eggs, salt and pepper; whisk to combine thoroughly.

Step 3. Make 6 sandwiches layering 1 slice ham, 1 slice turkey and 1 slice cheese (can use more more).

Step 4. Lightly brush the outside of the sandwiches with melted butter.

Step 5. Melt butter in a skillet over low heat.

Step 6. Dip the sandwich/s in the milk/egg mixture, turning to coat each side.

Step 7. Brown in the skillet.

27. Heavenly Tailgate Club Sandwich

Yield: Makes 6 Servings
Ingredients:
1 loaf unsliced round bread (about 9" diameter)
1 cup bottled sour cream and bacon salad dressing
lettuce
1/3 lb. sliced Swiss cheese
3/4 lb. sliced cooked roast beef
1/2 lb. sliced cooked turkey
1 large tomatoes, sliced

To Make:

Step 1. Cut bread in half horizontally; hollow out center of each half, leaving 1/4 inch shell.

Step 2. Spread 1/3 cup of the sour cream and bacon dressing into each shell.

Step 3. Line bottom of each shell with lettuce.

Step 4. Into the bottom of each shell layer cheese, roast beef, remaining dressing, turkey and then tomato.

Step 5. Top with lettuce.

Step 6. Replace top shell.

Step 7. To serve, cut into wedges.

28. Inviting Turkey & Feta Grilled Sandwich

Yield: Makes 1 Serving
Ingredients:
2 slices smoked deli turkey
2 slices wheat bread
2 leaves lettuce
1 1/2 tablespoons crumbled feta cheese
1 tablespoon Italian salad dressing
1 tablespoon butter

To Make:

Step 1. Put turkey slices atop one bread slice; top with lettuce and feta cheese.

Step 2. Spread Italian salad dressing over one side of the second bread slice and lay atop the other slice with the dressing facing downward.

Step 3. Melt butter in a skillet over medium heat.

Step 4. Cook sandwich in melted butter until browned, about 2 minutes per side.

29. Tantalizing Smoked Turkey Sandwich With Cranberry Butter

Yield: Makes 4 Servings
Ingredients:
1/2 cup cranberries (may use frozen, but thaw and drain them)
3 tablespoons unsalted butter
1 teaspoon honey
1 teaspoon Dijon mustard
8 slices rye bread
1 lb. smoked turkey, thinly sliced
12 ounces jarlsberg cheese, thinly sliced
8 romaine lettuce leaves
cherry tomatoes (optional garnish)

To Make:

Step 1. Puree the cranberries with the butter, honey, and Dijon mustard in a food processor or a blender by whirling at high speed for about 1 minute.

Step 2. Spread on one side of each slice of bread.

Step 3. Stack the turkey, cheese, and lettuce on half of the bread slices, dividing the total amount evenly.

Step 4. Cover with the remaining bread slices.

Step 5. Halve diagonally, then garnish, if desired, with the cherry tomatoes.

30. Yummy Smoked Turkey & Stilton Sandwich

Yield: Makes 4 Servings
Ingredients:
6 ounces Stilton cheese, crumbled and softened
6 tablespoons mayonnaise
2 tablespoons bottled mango chutney (to taste)
1 -2 tablespoon minced fresh parsley leaves
fresh lemon juice, to taste
four 5-inch lengths Italian bread or French bread, halved horizontally and toasted
3/4 lb. smoked turkey breast, thinly sliced
arugula or lettuce leaf

To Make:

Step 1. In a small bowl mash together with a fork the Stilton, mayonnaise, chutney, parsley, lemon juice, and salt and pepper (to taste) until the mixture is combined well.

Step 2. Spread the halves of the bread with the Stilton mixture, and divide the turkey between the bottom halves of the bread.

Step 3. Top with the arugula and cover the sandwiches with the top halves of the bread.

31. Choice Grilled Hot Turkey Sandwiches

Yield: Makes 4 Servings
Ingredients:
4 tablespoons mayonnaise
2 tablespoons salsa
2 green onions, chopped
8 slices sourdough bread
1/2 pound deli-sliced turkey
4 slices Pepperjack cheese
4 tablespoons butter

To Make:

Step 1. Mix the mayonnaise, salsa, and green onions in a small bowl.

Step 2. Spread the seasoned mayonnaise evenly on each slice of bread.

Step 3. Layer the turkey and cheese on 4 of the slices.

Step 4. Top with remaining bread to make 4 sandwiches.

Step 5. Melt 2 tablespoons butter in a large skillet over medium heat.

Step 6. Fry sandwiches in butter until lightly toasted.

Step 7. Add remaining butter to skillet, turn sandwiches over.

Step 8. Cook until the cheese is melted, and the bread is browned.

32. Tasteful Toasted Turkey & Bacon Sandwiches

Yield: Makes 4 Servings
Ingredients:
2 tablespoons mayonnaise
1 tablespoon ranch dressing
8 slices soft Italian bread (about 1/2 in. thick)
4 ounces deli turkey (shaved from deli)
4 slices bacon, cooked and halved
4 slices tomatoes, halved
2 slices cheddar cheese, halved
2 tablespoons butter or 2 tablespoons margarine

To Make:
Step 1. In small bowl, mix mayonnaise and dressing.
Step 2. Spread on one side of each slice of bread.
Step 3. Top each of 4 bread slices with turkey, baconk, tomato, cheese and remaining bread slices, mayonnaise mixture side down.
Step 4. Spread butter on one side of each sandwich.
Step 5. In a 12 inches skillet, place sandwiches butter side down.
Step 6. Spread butter over top of each sandwich.
Step 7. Cover; cook over medium-low heat for 6-8 minutes or until bottoms are golden brown.
Step 8. Turn sandwiches; cover and cook 5-6 minutes longer or until bottoms are golden brown and cheese is melted.

33. Ambrosia Turkey Sandwiches With Cranberry Sauce

Yield: Makes 4 Servings
Ingredients:
1 loaf French bread
4 tablespoons margarine
8 ounces sliced deli turkey meat
8 slices provolone cheese
8 slices precooked bacon
4 tablespoons mayonnaise
4 tablespoons jellied cranberry sauce
8 slices fresh tomatoes
4 lettuce leaves

To Make:
Step 1. Preheat the oven broiler.
Step 2. Cut the bread into four pieces, and split lengthwise almost all the way through for four sandwiches.
Step 3. Spread margarine on the inside of each piece.
Step 4. Place on a baking sheet, cut side up.
Step 5. Toast bread under preheated broiler until lightly browned, 1 to 2 minutes.
Step 6. Remove pan from the oven.
Step 7. Layer 4 pieces of bread with 2 slices each of the turkey, cheese, and bacon.
Step 8. Remove the remaining 4 slices of bread from the baking sheet and reserve for sandwich tops.
Step 9. Cool bread slightly, and spread mayonnaise onto the cut side of each of the 4 top slices.
Step 10. Place the bread with turkey and cheese under the broiler just until the cheese melts, about 1 minute.
Step 11. Remove from the broiler, and spread 1 tablespoon cranberry sauce over each sandwich.
Step 12. Layer with the tomatoes and lettuce.
Step 13. Place a top bread slice over each half, and serve.

34. Tempting Turkey Tea Sandwiches

Yield: Makes 10 Servings
Ingredients:
1 (8 ounce) package cream cheese, room temperature
1/2 cup minced scallion (white and green parts)
1 loaf raisin nut bread
8 slices fresh turkey or 8 slices smoked turkey breast (thin slices)
fresh basil leaf

To Make:

Step 1. Mix the cream cheese and scallions together ahead of time so the flavors can blend.

Step 2. Lay out 8 slices of bread and spread them all with a thin layer of scallion cream cheese.

Step 3. Place a single layer of turkey on half the slices, cutting the edges to fit the bread.

Step 4. Place the basil leaves randomly on top of the turkey.

Step 5. Top with the other 4 slices of bread, cream cheese side down.

Step 6. Wrap and refrigerate until the cream cheese is cold and firm.

Step 7. Cut the sandwiches into whatever shapes desired.

Serve chilled.

35. Unimaginable Mom's Sit Sandwich

Yield: Makes 6 Servings
Ingredients:
1 large round loaf French bread (or oval "peasant" loaf, or sourdough)
1 (6 1/2 ounce) jar marinated artichoke hearts, drained, liquid reserved (you can use the hearts whole or roughly chopped)
1/2 cup mayonnaise
3 large ripe tomatoes, sliced
3 ounces thinly sliced salami
1/2 lb. thinly sliced unsmoked turkey breast
1/4 lb. cheese slice, any kind (provolone and fresh mozzarella are my favorite)
1 (2 1/2 ounce) can sliced ripe black olives, drained
1 purple onion, thinly sliced (amount to taste)
To Make:
Step 1. Cut loaf of bread in half horizontally and hollow out the soft bread from both halves, leaving a shell about 3/4-inch thick.
Step 2. Reserve soft bread for another use.
Step 3. In small bowl, combine artichoke liquid with mayonnaise and spread onto bread shells.
Step 4. In bottom half, layer ingredients at least three times until mounded high, beginning and ending with tomatoes.
Step 5. Place top half of bread over mound of ingredients.

Step 6. Wrap entire loaf tightly with plastic wrap.
This must be assembled at least 2 hours before serving, but can be assembled up to 8 hours before serving.

Step 7. Refrigerate.
Before serving, place sandwich (wrapped in plastic) on a hard surface and SIT ON IT! This smashes the ingredients together and makes it easier to serve. Do not omit this step, strange as it seems, as this step is what makes the sandwich delicious.
Step 8. Slice the loaf into wedges or slices to serve.
Note:#1: I usually roughly chop the artichoke hearts, myself. Also, regarding the artichoke juice mixture: you can add only half of it to the mayo, if you like - how much of the spread you're going to need depends on the size of loaf you've gotten.
Note #2: other good additions I've made to the sandwich include strips of roasted red and yellow pepper, whole fresh basil leaves (placed on top of the tomatoes) or pesto into the mayo, pepperoncini and/or sliced sweet red cherry peppers, pancetta, and more salami or other hard sausage than the recipe calls for.
Note #3: any leftover mayo mixture, by the way, makes a great salad dressing! I once accidentally used the juice from a jar larger than the recipe called for and the mixture was far more than I needed -- so to thicken it up a bit I added a bit of low fat sour cream, and made the leftover mixture (much to my husband's delight) available as salad dressing. Yum!

36. A Shocker Pink Turkey Sandwich

Yield: Makes 1 Serving
Ingredients:
2 slices white bread
2 slices deli turkey
1 tablespoon strawberry cream cheese
1 lettuce leaf
To Make:
Step 1. Spread strawberry cream cheese on one slice of bread.
Step 2. Put lettuce on other slice of bread.
Step 3. Put turkey in between the lettuce and cream cheese.

37. Gotta Have It Jamaican Turkey Sandwich

Yield: Makes 6 Servings
Ingredients:
Pulled Turkey:
1/2 cup chopped celery
1/3 cup chopped green onion
1 (2 pound) skinless, boneless turkey breast, cut into 8 ounce chunks
1/2 cup juice from canned pineapple
1/4 cup sweet chili sauce
3 tablespoons distilled white vinegar
2 tablespoons water
1 tablespoon beef bouillon granules
2 teaspoons garlic powder
6 canned pineapple rings
Coleslaw Topping:
1/4 cup mayonnaise
1 tablespoon lemon juice
2 tablespoons chopped fresh parsley
1/2 cup chopped onion
2 cups chopped cabbage
1 cup shredded Cheddar cheese
salt and black pepper to taste
6 Kaiser rolls, split
To Make:
Step 1. Sprinkle the celery and green onions into the bottom of a slow cooker; place the turkey chunks on top.

Step 2. Combine the pineapple juice, sweet chili sauce, vinegar, water, beef bouillon, and garlic powder; pour over the turkey.

Step 3. Place the pineapple rings on the turkey chunks.

Step 4. Cook on Low until the turkey pulls apart easily, 6 to 7 hours.

Step 5. Meanwhile, make the coleslaw by stirring the mayonnaise, lemon juice, parsley, and onion together in a mixing bowl.

Step 6. Add the cabbage and Cheddar cheese; season to taste with salt and pepper.

Step 7. Cover, and refrigerate while the turkey cooks.

Step 8. Once the turkey is tender, shred using two forks.

Step 9. Pile some of the shredded turkey and a pineapple ring onto a Kaiser roll; top with coleslaw to serve.

1) The Best Ham And Cheese Sandwich

Prep Time: 20 minutes
Cook Time: 30 minutes
Ready In: 1 hour
Servings: 4 sandwiches
INGREDIENTS:
¼ cup heavy whipping cream
¼ tsp. ground cinnamon
2 pinch cayenne pepper
1 pinch kosher salt
1 pinch salt
1 tbsp. butter
1 tbsp. white sugar
1/8 tsp. ground allspice
2 large eggs
2 tsp. chopped fresh chives
4 slices Cheddar cheese
4 slices Havarti cheese
4 thick slices day-old French bread
8 poached eggs
8 thin slices cooked ham

DIRECTIONS:
1. Mix together white sugar, cream, and 2 eggs in a bowl. Add cinnamon, 1 pinch of cayenne pepper, salt and allspice. Whisk until fully incorporated. Set aside.
2. Preheat oven to 375F. Meanwhile, prepare the bread. Place each bread slices into the batter 10 minutes per side or until the bread has fully absorbed the batter.
3. After that, melt butter in a large skillet over medium heat. Put bread slices into the melted butter and cook until browned for about 2 to 3 minutes per side. Drain excess oil of the toast into a baking sheet.
4. After all the bread slices are done, cook ham into the same skillet until brown or about 1 minute per side of the ham. Transfer into a baking sheet to drain excess oil.
5. Now to assemble the sandwich, lay French toast on a cookie sheet. Top it with Cheddar cheese then place 2 slices of ham over it. Cover ham with the Havarti cheese. Place arranged sandwiches into the preheated oven and bake it for about 20 minutes or when the toast are no longer wet and cheese has melted and begun to brown.
6. Transfer sandwiches on a serving plate and top it each with 2 poached eggs. Sprinkle a kosher salt and another pinch of cayenne pepper. Serve and enjoy.

2)Hearty Breakfast Sandwich

Prep Time: 20 minutes
Cook Time: 20 minutes
Ready In: 40minutes
Servings: 6
INGREDIENTS:
¼ cup milk
½ cup chopped green bell pepper
½ cup chopped onion
1 cup sliced mushrooms
3 slices bacon
6 eggs
6 Kaiser Rolls, split
6 thin slices ham
6 thin slices Swiss or Muenster cheese
6 thin slices tomato

DIRECTIONS:
1. Place a large non-stick skillet over medium heat. Fry bacon until crisp then drain excess oil. Allow to cool for a few minutes then crumble it. Set aside.
2. Using the same skillet, place the mushroom, bell pepper and onion and sauté for about 5 minutes or until tender. Mix in the crumbled bacon and continue cooking.
3. Meanwhile, combine milk and egg in a medium bowl then whisk them together until blended. Add the egg mixture into the skillet and cook until it begins to set. Pull the eggs across the pan and fold.
4. Continue cooking, pulling, lifting and folding again the eggs until thickened and no longer wet. Do not stir.
5. To arrange the sandwich, lay bottom rolls in a cookie sheet, spoon each rolls with the egg mixture. Place slice of ham, tomato then cheese over the egg. Broil sandwich for 3 minutes 6" from heat just until the cheese is melted. Cover with roll tops then serve.

3) Mini Pizza's With Scrambled Egg

Prep Time: 10 minutes
Ready In: 10 minutes
Servings: 1

INGREDIENTS:
1 large egg, beaten
1 whole-wheat English muffin
2 slices pepperoni
2 tbsp. prepared marinara sauce
2 tbsp. shredded Italian cheese blend

DIRECTIONS:

1. Split English muffin then toastand set aside. Preheat oven or toaster oven broiler.
2. Place a small non-stick skillet over medium-high heat. Grease the skillet with a cooking spray then add the egg and cook for 1 to 2 minutes or until set into soft curds. Stir frequently.
3. Coat halves of English muffin with marinara sauce. Place scrambled egg on the top of the muffin. Add cheese and pepperoni. Cover with the other halves of the muffin and broil for 1 to 3 minutes, just until the cheese is melted.
4. Serve!

4) Cheesy Buttered Breakfast Sandwich

Prep Time: 6 minutes
Cook Time: 4 minutes
Ready In: 10minutes
Servings: 1
INGREDIENTS:
2 slices American cheese
2 slices of bread
Butter

DIRECTIONS:
1. Cut each bread slices into 4" circles then softened the butter. Coat the butter into one side of each bread circle and set aside.
2. Meanwhile, prepare a Breakfast Sandwich Maker. Preheat it until the green light comes on.
3. Lift the cover, top ring and cooking plate of the Sandwich Maker. Then place one bread circle in the bottom ring of Breakfast Maker with the buttered-side down. Place the cheese on top then lower the cooking plate and top ring.

4. Add another bread circle with the buttered-side on top into the cooking plate. Close cover and cook for 3 to 4 minutes. After that, rotate the handle clockwise to slide out the cooking plate. Lift the cover and rings then carefully remove the sandwich with plastic spatula.
5. Serve.

5)Cheesy Baguette With Basil And Egg

Prep Time: 10 minutes
Ready In: 10 minutes
Servings: 1
INGREDIENTS:
¼ cup fresh basil leaves
1 piece (6" long) baguette
1 tsp. butter
2 large eggs
2 large tomato slices
2 slices cheddar cheese
Coarse salt
Freshly ground pepper

DIRECTIONS:
1. Set oven to 350F then leave to heat.
2. For the meantime, prepare the sandwich. Slice baguette horizontally. Once the oven is ready, lightly toast the bread until cut sides up.
3. Place 1 slice of cheese on each side of the bread then continue cooking in the oven for about 1 to 2 minutes, until the cheese melts.
4. While waiting, melt butter in a skillet then fry the eggs. Sprinkle it with salt and pepper. Once the egg is cooked, place it on bottom half of the bread. Top it with tomatoes and basil.
5. Cover the bread with the other half of the bread and press down slightly. Wrap tightly in parchment or serve immediately.

6)Bacon, Omelette And Tomato English Muffin

Prep Time: 15 minutes
Cook Time: 30 minutes
Ready In: 45minutes
Servings: 4
INGREDIENTS:
¼ cup chives, minced
¼ cup parsley, minced
1 large beefsteak tomato
4 1/2" round slice Canadian bacon
4 egg whites
4 eggs
4 whole-wheat English muffins
Non-stick cooking spray

DIRECTIONS:

1. Combine egg whites and egg into a bowl then whisk to combine. Add in the parsley and chives then continue stirring until fully blended with the eggs.

2. Grease with cooking spray a large skillet then ladle about ¼ of the egg mixture and pour it into the skillet. Cook the egg mixture, omelette style for 1 to 2 minutes until egg is cooked through.

3. Once cooked, transfer the egg into a plate and cover with foil to keep it warm. Then, repeat the procedures with the remaining egg mixture. Once the egg mixture is done, heat the Canadian bacon into the same skillet for 1-2 minutes per side or until warm.

4. Toast the English muffin for a few minutes. While waiting for the muffins, gently fold the omelette to fit into the muffin. Then put omelette on one half of muffin then top it with bacon slice and tomato. Cover it with the other half of the muffin. Press gently and serve

7) Avocado And Egg Breakfast Sandwich

Prep Time: 15 minutes
Cook Time: 5 minutes
Ready In: 20 minutes
Servings: 1
INGREDIENTS:
½ of ripe avocado, mashed
1 egg
1 tbsp. basil, chopped
1 tsp. coconut oil
1 tsp. mayonnaise
2 slices English muffin
Pepper
Salt

DIRECTIONS:

1. Fry egg "sunny side-up" in coconut oil then sprinkle chopped basil on top while cooking. Season it with salt and pepper.

2. Meanwhile, while waiting for the egg to cooked, toast the muffin slices. Then spread one slice of mayonnaise into the toasted muffin.

3. Mash the avocado slices then place it on the other side of the muffin toast. Place the medium cooked egg in between slices and serve.

8)Energizing Egg Breakfast Sandwich

Prep Time: 10 minutes
Cook Time: 5 minutes
Ready In: 15 minutes
Servings: 1

INGREDIENTS:
½ cup fresh spinach leaves
1 egg, cooked (poached, scrambled or fried)
1 slice tomato
1 tsp. I Can't Believe It's Not Butter Spread
2 slices whole wheat bread

DIRECTIONS:

1. Wash spinach leaves, rinsed then patted it to dry. Slice it thinly and set aside.
2. Toast bread slices then spread it evenly with butter. Place cooked egg and tomato on top of one slice of the toast.
3. Sprinkle it with spinach and top it with the other slice of the toast. Serve.

9) Sautéed Spinach, Mushroom And Egg Breakfast Sandwich

Prep Time: 25 minutes
Ready In: 25minutes
Servings: 2

INGREDIENTS:
2 cups loosely packed baby spinach
2 eggs
2 English muffins split in half
2 ounces smoked ham, thinly sliced
3 ½ tbsp. vegetable oil, divided
4 slices of bacon
4 tbsp. salted butter, softened and divided
5 cremini mushrooms, cleaned and thinly sliced
Salt and pepper to taste

DIRECTIONS:

1. Spread 1 tablespoon of melted butter into each slices of muffins. Place muffins cut-side down into a skillet over medium-high heat. Toast it for 4-5 minutes or until golden brown. Turn over to cook the other side of the muffin for another 2 minutes then set aside.

2. Using the same skillet, sauté mushrooms with 1 tablespoon of vegetable oil. Add salt and pepper. Stir for a few seconds, remove then set aside. Pour another ½ tbsp. of vegetable oil into the skillet and sauté spinach for 2-3 minutes or until wilted. Transfer into a small bowl and set also aside.

3. Now, cook bacon into the skillet for 4-5 minutes or until brown then flip over and cook for another 2-3 minutes until crisp. Place on paper towels to drain and set aside.

4. Cook ham for 1 minute in each side into the skillet using only about 2 tbsp. of the remaining oil. Place it also into the paper towels together with the bacons. Then fry eggs for 3 minutes. Add oil if needed. Stab the yolks with a fork then flip and fry for another 2 minutes then flip and fry again for 1 minute. Season it with salt and pepper if desired.

5. Once all ingredients are done, arrange the sandwich. Place ham into 2 muffin halves, cut-side-up. Then top it with bacon followed by spinach then mushroom and last the fried egg. Cover it with the other halves of the muffins. Press it down gently to secure and serve.

10) Sauerkraut And Egg Gluten-Free Breakfast Sandwich

Prep Time: 3 minutes
Cook Time: 10 minutes
Ready In: 13minutes
Servings: 1
INGREDIENTS:
1 garlic clove, sliced thin
1 thick slice tomato
2 eggs
2 slices coconut Paleo Bread
2 tbsp. Sauerkraut
Coconut oil
Salt and pepper to taste

DIRECTIONS:

1. Melt coconut oil into a pan then cook eggs according to your liking. Add garlic slices then cook depending on your preferred outcome of the garlic.

2. Toast Paleo Bread then place eggs with garlic into one side of the bread. Top it with tomato then sauerkraut. Sprinkle it with salt and pepper. Serve.

11) Cheesy Onion And Italian Sausage Breakfast Sandwich

Prep Time: 30 minutes
Ready In: 30minutes
Servings: 8 sandwiches
INGREDIENTS:
For Bread:
12 oz. beer or soda water
Full box Beer Bread Mix
For Sandwiches:
1 cup green onion, finely chopped
1 lbs. spicy or sweet Italian sausage
8 large eggs
8 oz. Monterey Jack Cheese, shredded
8 slices Classic Beer Bread
8 tbsp. extra-virgin olive oil
Salt and pepper

DIRECTIONS:
1. Prepare the Beer Bread according to package direction then make 8 slices. Preheat oven to 400F then place bread slices onto a baking sheet and cover it with shredded cheese. Set aside.
2. Mix together 6 tablespoon of olive oil with onions, salt and pepper then spread it evenly into the bread slices. Place a large skillet over medium-high heat then sauté Italian sausage until cooked.
3. Divide sausages and top it into the bread slices. Put the baking sheet into the preheated oven then bake it for about 8-10 minutes or until cheese melts and bread begins to crisp around edges.
4. While waiting, place 2 large skillets over medium-high heat then pour 1 tablespoon of oil. Crack 4 eggs in each skillet and cook for 2 minutes. Add salt and pepper to taste. Remove from heat then once the bread is done, top 1 egg over each slice of bread. Serve.

12) Cream Cheese Salmon With Spinach And Egg Breakfast Sandwich

Prep Time: 5 minutes
Ready In: 5minutes
Servings: 1
INGREDIENTS:
1 egg white
Crackled pepper
English muffin
Salmon flavored cream cheese
Spinach leaves
Tomato slice

DIRECTIONS:
1. Toast bread then set aside.
2. Place egg whites into a coffee mug then baked it for 15-20 seconds or until egg whites are no longer runny.
3. Then spread each slice of the bread with salmon flavoured cream cheese. Top one slice of bread with the egg white followed by the spinach leaves then the tomato and sprinkles it with cracked pepper.
4. Cover with the other piece of the bread and serve.

13) Avocado, Arugula And Egg Sandwich

Prep Time: 6 minutes
Ready In: 6minutes
Servings: 2
INGREDIENTS:
½ cup of arugula
1 avocado, cut into 4 equal parts
4 large eggs
4 slices of bread, toasted
Salt and pepper
Lemon, or olive oil

DIRECTIONS:

1. Arrange toasted bread on a plate. Then cook eggs according to your desired cooking style.
2. Spread ¼ avocados on each slice of the toast then top it with arugula. Place egg over it. Add salt and pepper.
3. Squeeze lemon or drizzle it with olive oil before serving. Enjoy!

14) Avocado, Bacon, Tomato And Egg Breakfast Sandwich

Prep Time: 15 minutes
Ready In: 15 minutes
Servings: 2 sandwiches

INGREDIENTS:
½ large Hass avocado
10-12 cherry tomatoes
2 eggs
2 slices thick cut bacon
2 tsp. lemon juice
4 thick slices of Batard
Freshly ground black pepper
Table or fine sea salt

DIRECTIONS:
1. Cook bacon into a cold frying pan over medium heat until crisp. Turn occasionally until fully cooked. Transfer cooked bacon on a plate lined with paper towel to drain excess oil. Crumble bacon and set aside.
2. Mix avocado with lemon juice and ¼ tsp. of salt. Whisk mixture until fairly smooth then set aside. Wash then slice cherry tomatoes into quarters and set aside. Toast bread and crack eggs into a small bowl. Set also aside.
3. Place eggs into the frying pan. Add salt and pepper. Cook eggs for a few minutes or until whites are set but the yolks are still runny.
4. Arrange the sandwich by dividing mashed avocado and tomato between the 4 slices of bread. Spread

avocado into each slice then top it with the tomato. Sprinkle with salt, pepper and crumpled bacon the top of bread slices. Add egg then serve.

15) Hash Brown Patty With Spinach And Cheese Sandwich

Prep Time: 5 minutes
Cook Time: 10 minutes
Ready In: 15 minutes
Servings: 4

INGREDIENTS:
½ tsp. salt
1 package (8oz.) Rondele garlic cheese spread
1 pound ham, sliced thinly
1 tbsp. chives, chopped
1 tsp. butter
1 tsp. vinegar
1 vine-ripened tomato, sliced
2 cups spinach leaves
2 tbsp. vegetable oil
4 eggs
4 slice brie cheese
8 frozen hash brown patties

DIRECTIONS:
1. Preheat oven to 350F. Meanwhile, place a non-stick skillet over medium heat. Fry hash browns until brown and crisp. Set aside but keep it warm.
2. Melt butter in a skillet then sauté spinach. Add salt then allow it cool for a few minutes. Squeeze out excess liquid from the spinach and set aside.
3. Crack eggs into a small bowl. Then pour water in a pot then mix in with vinegar. Allow to simmer then

gently slide eggs one at a time. Poach eggs for 2-3 minutes until set. Then drain and set aside.

4.In an oven-proof serving plate, arrange 1 piece of hash brown then spread garlic cheese spread evenly over the top of it. Place ¼ sautéed spinach on top; add the sliced tomato, brie cheese and the sliced ham in order.

5.Cover it with the second hash brown and the poached egg. Place in the oven for 5 minutes until warm then sprinkle it with chopped knives before serving.

16) Hearty Meatless Breakfast Sandwich

Prep Time: 5 minutes
Cook Time: 5 minutes
Ready In: 10 minutes
Servings: 2

INGREDIENTS:

½ tsp. smoked paprika
1 tsp. vegetable oil
2 ciabatta rolls, halved
2 large eggs
4 large tomato slices
4 slices cheddar cheese
Ground black pepper
Salt

DIRECTIONS:

1. Place a small non-stick skillet over medium heat. Pour oil then allow it to heat before cracking the eggs over it. Break the egg yolks then sprinkle it with salt and pepper. Add smoked paprika then cover. Cook the eggs for 2 minutes or until set.
2. Flip eggs over then season the other side. Cook for another 2 minutes. For the meantime, broil the ciabatta until golden brown. Sprinkle tomato slices with salt then add it into the ciabatta together with cheese. Continue broiling until cheese is melted.
3. Arrange the ciabatta then top with egg the tomato and cheese and cover it with the other slice of ciabatta. Serve.

17) Sausage, Bacon, And Avocado Breakfast Sandwich

Prep Time: 10 minutes
Cook Time: 10 minutes
Ready In: 20 minutes
Servings: 5 sandwiches

INGREDIENTS:
8 pieces bacon
5 eggs
5 (1 pound) Garlic Meyers Sausage
2 avocados
10 pieces of Gluten Free Bread

DIRECTIONS:

1. Preheat oven to 350F. Then, gently grease a cookie sheet with cooking spray and arrange sausage. Place it into the oven and bake for 45 minutes.
2. Meanwhile, slice 8 bacons in half to make 16 pieces of bacon. Fry it until crisp and set aside.
3. Toast the bread then fry the eggs. Once sausage is ready, cut it into 3 pieces horizontally. Place it on top of the toasted bread vertically. Top it with fried egg. Cover it with bacon horizontally. And lastly, place avocado slices on top and the other side of the toasted bread.
4. Wrap it with foil then place it on the grill to heat then serve. Enjoy!

18) Baked Egg And Spinach With Avocado Bagel Sandwich

Prep Time: 8 minutes
Ready In: 8 minutes
Servings: 1

INGREDIENTS:
¾ cup egg whites
1 Thomas Everything Bagel Thin
1 wedge Laughing Cow Herb & Garlic Cheese
10-15 fresh spinach leaves
2 slices tomato
2-4 slices avocado
Cholula hot sauce
Kosher salt

DIRECTIONS:
1.Toast the bagel in the oven then set it aside.
2.Combine egg whites and spinach leaves in a small bowl. Add kosher salt and mix them altogether. Put inside the microwave for 1 minute and 30 seconds. Check eggs to avoid overflowing.
3.Place cheese on toasted bagel and top it with tomato. Remove egg from the bowl then place it on top of the tomato. Add avocado and season it with more salt. Drizzle it with hot sauce then cover it with another slice of bagel and serve.

19) Toasted Baguette With Mixed Greens, Avocado And Egg Sandwich

Prep Time: 15 minutes
Ready In: 15 minutes
Servings: 2 sandwiches
INGREDIENTS:
½ avocado, pitted and skinned
1 baguette
2-3 tbsp. mayonnaise
3 hardboiled eggs, shelled
Gherkins
Handful of mixed greens
Micro greens
Red onions
Salt and pepper
DIRECTIONS:

1. Slice baguette in half with ends removed and toast it lightly. Slice thinly the avocado, egg, red onions and gherkins. Set aside.
2. Coat one side of 2 slices of toasted baguette. Place on top of it the mixed greens, avocado slices and egg slices in order. Sprinkle salt and pepper to taste.
3. Add red onions on top of the eggs, then the micro greens and the gherkins. Cover the sandwich with other slices of toasted baguette. Gently press down the sandwich and serve.

20) Toasted Croissants With Buttered Egg And Bean Sprouts

Prep Time: 10 minutes
Cook Time: 8 minutes
Ready In: 18 minutes
Servings: 2 croissant sandwiches

INGREDIENTS:
½ avocado, sliced
½ tomato, sliced
2 croissants (bakery made)
4 eggs, fried
Bean sprouts
Butter
Cheddar cheese, grated
Pepper
 Red onion, sliced
Salt

DIRECTIONS:
1. Preheat oven to 400F. Slice croissant in half. Arrange it on a baking sheet face-down and toast it for 5 minutes.
2. Once croissant slices are set, flip them and arrange the fillings. Sprinkle some grated cheese on the top part of the croissant and avocado, onion and tomato on the bottom part.
3. Place it back into the oven and bake it for 4 minutes and serve.

21) Asparagus With Fried Egg Breakfast Sandwich

Prep Time: 10 minutes
Ready In: 10 minutes
Servings: 1

INGREDIENTS:
¼ avocado, sliced
½ tomatoes
1 egg
2 slices of multigrain bread
2-3 slices Serrano ham
3-4 asparagus
Extra-virgin olive oil

DIRECTION:
1. Pour oil into the pan and bring it to heat. Fry ham and asparagus until done. Remove from the pan and set aside.
2. Fry egg in the same pan then set it also aside. Sprinkle some olive oil into the bread and place a dab of butter on top. Toast the bread then arrange in a plate.
3. Place tomato on 1 slice of a toasted bread. Then place avocado, ham, and fried egg on top. Place asparagus then cover it with the other slice of the bread. Serve and enjoy!

22) Tangy Feta Cheese Over English Muffin

Prep Time: 5 minutes
Cook Time: 5 minutes
Ready In: 10 minutes
Servings: 2-4

INGREDIENTS:

½ cup feta cheese, crumbled
1 avocado, halved, pitted, peeled and diced
2 tbsp. butter
4 oz. smoked salmon- thinly diced
4 regular or whole wheat English muffins
4 tbsp. milk
6 large eggs
Chopped chives or fresh dill
Salt and pepper to taste

DIRECTIONS:

1. Arrange English muffins in a toaster then toast it.
2. Meanwhile, combine egg and milk. Whisk evenly to blend. Place a non-stick skillet over medium-low heat. Melt in the butter then cook the egg for about 3-4 minutes. Turn the heat off then mix in the feta cheese.
3. Transfer muffins on a plate then arrange scrambled egg on top. Place diced avocado and smoked salmon on top of the egg. Finish it with sprinkling chopped chives or dill all over top.
4. Best serve with coffee. Enjoy!

23) Low Calorie Breakfast Sandwich

Prep Time: 5 minutes
Cook Time: 10 minutes
Ready In: 15 minutes
Servings: 2

INGREDIENTS:
1 medium muffin, halved
2 medium eggs
2 tbsp. low-fat crème fraiche
2 tbsp. vinegar
200g frozen spinach
Freshly grated nutmeg
Freshly ground black pepper
Salt

DIRECTIONS:
1. Fill a pan with water and boil it with vinegar. While waiting for the water to boil, toast muffin halves until lightly browned. Then set aside.
2. In a saucepan, heat spinach and add salt and pepper to taste. Mix in the nutmeg and crème fraiche. Set aside.
3. Crack eggs into a small cup. Once the water in the pan is boiling, gently slide each egg into the boiling water one at a time. Reduce heat then simmer for 3 minutes each until white has set and firm but yolks are still soft and runny.
4. Place spinach on top of the muffin halves. Add poached egg over the spinach. Sprinkle with salt and ground black pepper. Serve immediately.

www.ingramcontent.com/pod-product-compliance
Lightning Source LLC
Chambersburg PA
CBHW071441070526
44578CB00001B/174